A gift from
The Friends of the
Saint Paul Public Library

MONG EDUCATION AT THE CROSSROADS

Paoze Thao

University Press of America,® Inc.
Lanham • New York • Oxford

University Press of America,® Inc.
4720 Boston Way
Lanham, Maryland 20706

12 Hid's Copse Rd.
Cumnor Hill, Oxford OX2 9JJ

Library of Congress Cataloging-in-Publication Data

Thao, Paoze.
Mong education at the crossroads / Paoze Thao.
p.   cm.
Includes bibliographical references and index.
1. Hmong Americans—Education—Social aspects. 2. Hmong
(Asian people)—History. I. Title.
LC350l.H56T53 1999 371.829'95942—dc21   99—21902 CIP

ISBN 0-7618-1399-3 (cloth: alk. ppr.)

∞™ The paper used in this publication meets the minimum
requirements of American National Standard for Information
Sciences—Permanence of Paper for Printed Library Materials,
ANSI Z39.48—1984

To

Gonggi Xiong Thao

my wife

PREFACE

From antiquity to the present, Mong history and experiences have been recorded and shared mostly by western scholars or Chinese intellectuals. There is very little historical evidence suggesting that the Mong themselves have attempted to tell their own stories in their own versions from their own perspectives. This is due to the fact that the Mong did not have a writing system of their own until recently. The majority of Mong-Americans have been illiterate in their own language as well as in other languages. This book, *Mong Education at the Crossroads*, was written by the author to tell the Mong story from the perspective of a Mong-American. This manuscript evolved from the extensive research cited in the author's study, *Mong Resettlement in the United States (1978-1987): Educational Implications*, conducted at Loyola University of Chicago in 1994. However, the contents of the manuscript were fully revised to reflect the up-to-date issues relating to the Mong-Americans and their experiences in the United States.

As the prospectus of this book has grown into a manuscript, I have renewed my firm commitment to work for my humanistic interpretations of the Mong educational experiences as they apply to the present conditions of the Mong-Americans in the United States. My work on this book reaffirms my belief that the history of the Mong and their educational experiences are valuable, cultural, and professional components not only for the Mong and Mong professionals but also for the society at large as well.

This book is intended to help educators understand the historical background and the educational experiences that the Mong-Americans have encountered throughout the series of formative episodes up to 1997. This book will examine the Mong-American experience through education. As recent immigrants in a new society, the Mong-Americans have encountered tremendous social and educational problems during their transition from Mong to Mong-Americans in the United States. Suggestions will also be made on how to address the cultural and educational issues faced by the Mong-Americans. This book is designed to be used as a textbook for courses in Southeast Asian history and culture, culture and cultural diversity, Mong history and education, comparative education, social and cultural foundations of education, and in Mong ethnic studies.

Acknowledgments

I am very grateful for the interest and continued support provided by Dr. Dorothy M. Lloyd, Dean of the Center for Collaborative Education and Professional Studies, and by my colleagues at California State University, Monterey Bay (CSUMB).

The initial development of this book was made possible by several channels of support throughout its writing. First, I want to thank Minerva Coyne, Director of the Multifunctional Resource Center (MRC) for Bilingual Education, Wisconsin Center for Education Research (WCER), School of Education, University of Wisconsin-Madison (UW-M), for her tremendous support between 1993-1995. During my tenure as Training and Research Specialist, I was asked to give a keynote presentation on "Mong Education at the Crossroads: Implications for Mong Children and Families" at the 1994 Statewide Conference on Equity and Multicultural Education, Stevens Point, Wisconsin on November 9, 1994. The preparation of that presentation was supported by the U.S. Department of Education under contract number T292013001 through funds provided by the Office of Bilingual Education and Minority Languages Affairs (OBEMLA) and by WCER, School of Education, UW-M.

Second, the author was awarded an Affirmative Action Faculty Development Grant from California State University, Monterey Bay in the Spring Semester of 1996 to provide services to the community. This partial mini-grant led me to refine the keynote address mentioned above to produce a video on "Mong Education at the Crossroads: Needs for Professional Development." The manuscript which was put together in videotape format was first presented at the Second Hmong National Conference in Sacramento on May 5, 1996. That video is currently used to supplement my current instructional support.

Third, I wish to express my appreciation to Dr. Harold M. Murai, who encouraged me to develop a course on Southeast Asians at California State University, Monterey Bay (CSUMB). With his encouragement, the two aforementioned presentations were expanded and materialized into this book.

Fourth, I am extremely indebted and privileged to have Dr. Christine E. Sleeter and Dr. Chris T. Hasegawa read and review this entire manuscript for this edition. Their valuable comments provided me with perspectives into my own writing and the problems of historical and comparative interpretations. I have been educated by their insightful comments and cannot thank them enough for their valuable time and suggestions. Not only did they generate valuable comments but their suggestions helped me solidify my own thought. Although I have incorporated the majority of their comments into this book, I have gone in my own way in a number of instances. The errors of fact, argument, interpretation, and recommendations remain in this book are mine alone. I want to thank my students who have always been a source of inspiration and stimulation for the development of this book. I would also like to thank E. Stephen Voss, President and Chief Executive Officer of International Institute of Los Angeles, for his assistance in editing this manuscript. Many thanks also go to Yer Thao who read the entire manuscript and provided me with very insightful comments and Dr. Marium Pendercamp of Humboldt State University for reading a few chapters of the manuscript.

All of the support mentioned above stems from my interest in developing and writing this manuscript to be used as a textbook for the course LS 362: Southeast Asian History and Culture. CSUMB began offering this course in the Fall Semester, 1996.

The process of writing this book was long and fatiguing, but a very rewarding experience for someone like the author who speaks English as his fifth language. The completion of this manuscript could not have been accomplished without the training in the historical and comparative method I received from Professors Gerald L. Gutek and Janis Fine of Loyola University of Chicago.

I am also indebted to my cousin, Pha Thao, for designing the cover for this book. He has always been the sources of my motivation and has supported my work. Finally, I am most gratified to my family. My wife, Gonggi, has always provided me with an atmosphere conducive to my work. To my children, Thongteng, Gaozong, Chee-Ah C. and Alexander Dhotzu, I send my love and gratitude.

Though the initial support for the preparation of this book was from the MRC, WCER, UW-M through funds provided by the Office of Bilingual Education and Minority Language Affairs (OBEMLA), U.S. Department of Education and California State University Monterey Bay (CSUMB), the opinions expressed in this manuscript are those of the author and do not necessarily reflect the views of MRC (WCER, UW-M), OBEMLA, and CSUMB.

TABLE OF CONTENTS

List of Tables

Introduction

"We didn't do very well with the Mong because we didn't have a teacher that can speak the language and also we didn't have a teacher who can speak Lao, Cambodian, and Vietnamese. The only thing that most of them have in common was that they were Buddhists so we use that as a commonality. They were given English as a Second Language and dumped into the same class. Eventually, we got a Vietnamese teacher and so the Vietnamese didn't go into that class. Eventually, we had a teacher who could speak Lao from Thailand and we kept the Mong in there any way because of the same nationality even though culture and language were different. It was also a question of space. We didn't have a special space to put them."[1]

When queried about how schools met the needs of the Mong students, this was a response from a coordinator of an English as a Second Language (ESL) program in a public school in Chicago.

This is a typical response we normally get from school officials. Schools, all of a sudden, have had an unexpected influx of many immigrant children. After the US withdrawal of its troops from Southeast Asia and after the fall of the Cambodian, Laotian and Vietnamese governments to the Communists since 1975, it is estimated that 1,072,471 Southeast Asian refugees have arrived in the United States.[2] Of these refugees, 225,675 are from Laos[3] and of these the Mong account for over 80,000.

The Mong, a closely-knit ethnic hill tribe from Laos, originally migrated from China in the eighteenth century and settled in Southeast Asia. Those in Laos assisted France during its colonial rule and the United States in its Secret War against the Communists during the Vietnam conflict. After the United States withdrew its troops from Southeast Asia, the Mong in Laos were persecuted for political reasons by the Communist governments. In 1976, Congress recognized that the Mong had been employed by the Central Intelligence Agency (CIA) and authorized the State Department to admit some as refugees to the United States.

Because of their constant massive migration within and across borders, the Mong have experienced a series of formative episodes: with the Chinese, with French Colonialism, with the Vietnam conflict, and with the refugee camps in Thailand during their transition to resettlement in the US and other western countries. These formative episodes will be discussed as a background for this study.

It is estimated that over 80,000 Mong refugees have been resettled throughout the US since 1976. Their lives had been completely disrupted by the long wars in Laos. Since the Mong did not have a written language, they face even greater barrier than other immigrants in acquiring the basic English language skills, such as speaking, listening, reading, and writing. Consequently, these factors left them with very limited marketable skills to earn a living in highly technologically-developed nations, such as the US. Of all the recent immigrants to the US, the Mong were most likely the least technologically sophisticated and the least formally educated. As a result, they have faced notoriously difficult adjustment problems in almost every aspect of their lives in the US.

In this book, the author attempts to present and discuss several aspects of adjustment problems experienced by many refugees in the United States. However, the specific focus is limited to Mong education at the Crossroads. The study reported in this book employs historical and qualitative methodologies. The author hopes that this book will provide the reader with a microcosm of the Mong in the US. A word of caution: this experience may not necessarily represent the entire Mong population in the nation. However, the author intends to draw and substantiate a generalization of the Mong based upon the data collected, which reflect some of the most difficult adjustment problems of the entire Mong population during their transition from Mong to Mong-Americans.

Terminology

Throughout this book, several terms have been used to designate the group of people that make up the ethnic group referred to as Mong.

"Miao" was historically used by the Chinese and can be loosely translated as "barbarian." The use of that term might be explained as being related to the Annamese word, "Meau" for cat.[4] "Mong-tse" was used in old Chinese historical works which likened the Mong language to the howling or cry of the hyena.[5] M. Terrien explained the meaning of the Chinese character for "Meau," transliterating it to as a cat's head. Terrian also related the form "Meau" to agricultural activities, consisting of two parts: one for "plant" and the other for "field;" whereas *tse* may be translated as "child." As a result, "Meau-tse" means "son of the soil, the farmers, who do not belong to the 'Great Nation.'"[6] Schotter, in the Chinese Kweichow sense, designated "Meau" as all non-Chinese.[7]

Other researchers, such as Barney and Smalley,[8] Binney,[9] Haudricourt,[10] Savina,[11] and Smalley,[12] spelled the word "Meo" as spoken by the Lao and the Thai. However, all the terms mentioned above carry negative connotations. The Mong prefer to be called 'Mong' by the Blue Mong or 'Hmong' for the White Hmong although the origin of the word 'Mong' or 'Hmong' is itself unknown. The term 'Mong' or 'Hmong' refers to a classless egalitarian ethnic group whose constituents call themselves 'Mong' or 'Hmong,' as do other groups, e.g. Americans, French, Dutch, Chinese, Koreans, etc.

The Mong in the United States can be classified culturally and linguistically by two major groups: (1) *Mong Leng (Moob Leeg)*, also known as Blue Mong and (2) White Hmong *(Hmoob Dawb)*. The spelling of Mong (Moob) and Hmong (Hmoob) are interchangeable. White Hmong refers to the color of a ceremonial dress, and no negative connotation is attached to the term. Two terms have been used to call Mong Leng: "Blue Mong" and "Green Mong." The term "Green Mong" has a negative connotation. Those identified by that term find it objectionable and offensive, and are intimidated by its use. Historically, "Green Mong" was one of the subgroups of the Mong who anachronistically practiced a cult of cannibalism. It is in the opinion of the author that that particular subgroup of Mong is no longer in existence. The author will use the term *Mong Leng* or Blue Mong in place of "Green Mong" to refer to this group. The *Mong Leng* are proud of their true name which translates **"Veins of the Mong,"** implying that the Mong Leng carry the life blood of all Mong.

It is difficult to estimate an accurate count of the two Mongs. However, they may be roughly equal in numbers and population. The two dialects can be mutually and intelligibly understood by the members of the other group. The two groups can be compared to people who speak American English and British English with approximately thirty percent (30%) difference in ethno-culture and language. The two groups have interwoven their bonds through intermarriage for centuries but, surprisingly, have preserved their linguistic and cultural homogeneity, and have respected each other's differences. Both groups have lived with each other harmoniously for centuries. In fact, their patterns of interaction constitute a system of checks and balances within the Mong society. The social, religious, educational, and political system has its own dynamics that are absolutely symmetrical within the Mong society. However, Mong Leng call themselves "*Mong*" and White Mong "*Hmong*."

The author will use the spelling "Mong" exclusively as opposed to any other terms for a variety of reasons. First, the term, 'Miao,' 'Meau,' 'Mong-tse,' and 'Meo,' have negative connotations. The spelling 'Mong' does not deviate significantly from the original terms and maintains consistency in the spelling from the perspectives of historical and comparative linguistics. Therefore, these terms 'Miao,' 'Meau,' 'Mong-tse,' 'Meau-tse,' and 'Meo' should be derived to the spelling 'Mong' rather than 'Hmong.'

Second, in February 1982, General Vang Pao established the Hmong Language Council in response to the resolutions made during the two consecutive Hmong national conferences held in June, 1980 in Minneapolis, Minnesota and in December, 1980 in Santa Ana, California.[13] He appointed twelve members to the council: six members representing the Mong Leng (Blue Mong) community and six members from the Hmong Dawb (White Hmong) community. The author was one of the appointed members. The role of the council was to undertake research and to conduct studies to standardize the Mong language. The committee members met at the University of Minnesota in Minneapolis, Minnesota on August 12-14, 1982 through the sponsorship of the Center for Applied Linguistics, Washington, DC. Based on the committee's literary search in various libraries, and pursuant to lengthy discussions of the terms, 'Hmong' and 'Mong,' the committee agreed that it was necessary to change the spelling of the initial **Hm** to **Mh** and from **Hmong** to **Mhong** to simplify library listings.[14] Therefore, the term '**Mhong**' is not a misspelling but a term intended to be neutral, a term acceptable to the language committee of both Mong Leng (Blue Mong) and Hmong Dawb (White Hmong) at the 1982 Minnesota conference.

Third, the spelling of the term 'Hmong' only appeared in Laos since 1975,[15] and was based solely on the socio-political and economic factors rather than from coining it from academic disciplines, such as linguistics, phonetics and phonology, historical and comparative linguistics and etymology. In terms of phonology, the sound /h/ in Mong is considered a voiceless glottal glide and can be used as a semi-vowel in certain contexts. In English, there is an aspiration of a small puff of air occurring immediately following the articulation of the oral stop sounds: /p/, /t/, and /k/ if they are syllable initial. In the articulation of /h/ sound, there is no obstruction of the airstream in the oral cavity. Due to this reason, linguists consider this aspiration a minor aspect in English phonology. This means that the aspiration that takes place with those three sounds does not change the overall phonemic representation of the phonemes /p/, /t/, and /k/ within the phonological context.[16] By the same context, compared to the Mong language, the phonetic sounds [m] vs. [hm]; [n] vs. [hn]; [ml] vs. [hml] ; and [ny] vs. [hny] between Blue Mong and White Hmong do not change the phonemic representation of the phonemes /m/,/n/,/ml/ and /ny/ within the phonological context and the meanings of the words, e.g. *Mong/Hm*ong; nub/hnub (meaning 'sun'); mluav/hmluav (meaning smashed or bent), and nyuaj/hnyuaj (meaning difficult). Therefore, the pairs of sounds [m]/[hm], [n]/[hn], [ml]/[hml], and [ny]/[hny] in Mong are the allophones of the same phonemes /m/,/n/, /ml/, and /ny/ respectively. An allophone is defined as "a predictable phonetic variant of a phoneme.[17] Thus, the aspiration feature for these four pairs of sounds does not change the overall phonemic representation of these phonemes in Mong. For this reason, the term 'Hmong' is therefore spelled 'Mong.'

Fourth, the decision to use the spelling **"Mong"** is not new. Researchers, such as Lyman,[18] Xiong et al,[19] Thao[20] and Thao[21] have used the spelling 'Mong.' The spelling 'Mong' was derived from the terms 'Miao,' 'Meau,' 'Mong-tse,' 'Meau-tse,' and 'Meo.' They were coined historically, and 'Mong' has always been consistent from the field of historical and comparative linguistics and etymology. In addition, in terms of pragmatics, the Mong and non-Mong would spell 'Mong' with an initial /m/ sound rather than an /hm/ when hearing the term 'Mong' or 'Hmong' for the first time.

Fifth, the decision to change the spelling from **"Mhong"** to **"Mong"** will further simplify library listings. Researchers tend to examine their literary search with the initial 'm' for 'Mong' rather than 'hm' for 'Hmong.'

Sixth, the US government is sensitive to the naming issue. A neutral term, "Highlander," was coined to include the Mong/Hmong, Iu Mien, Lao Lue, Lahu, and Lao Theung.[22] The term Highlander connotes a broader definition to include all the minority ethnic groups who came from the highlands of Laos and classifies them all "under the same roof;" whereas the Lao or Laotians are labeled as "Lowlanders."

Seventh, "M" was designated by the US officials as the official acronym for "Mong." On July 22, 1995, in Denver, Colorado, Chee Yang, Colonel "Bill" F. Biladeaux, Christine Cook, and the American Tribute Committee with the cooperation of Colonel Frank Bales, Generals Harry C. Aderholt, Jim Hall, Steve Ritchie, Art Cornelius, and the Mong veterans nationwide put together a special tribute to commemorate the 40,000 Mong soldiers who died in the US Secret Army in Laos and 15,000 who were wounded at the line of duty between 1961-1975. This tribute commemorated the Mong for the first time in the history of the United States. An upper case "M" was posted on the hill behind the background of the stage on that day. The US officials declared that that upper case "M" represents the "Mong" people.[23]

The terms -- Miao, Meau, Miao-tse, Meau-tse, Meo, Mong, Hmong - which are Mong or Highlander -- have all been used to refer to the same group of people in the US -- which are the Mong. They may be used interchangeably. Nevertheless, the author prefers the term "Mong," and other terms will be used as references. Occasionally, the use of a Mong word or other foreign language words may be necessary. In those events, transliteration will be utilized for clarity purposes.

Organization and Methodology

Through use of historical and qualitative methods, this book examines two principal areas: resettlement and education. It is intended to help educators understand the major trends that shaped the Mong society and their problems of cultural and educational adjustment during their resettlement in the United States. As a people, the Mong experienced a series of formative episodes: with the Chinese, with French Colonialism, with the Vietnam Conflict, with the refugee camps during their transition to resettlement in the United States.

This book consists of an introduction, seven chapters, a list of available resources with grade level appropriate reference materials, and an index section for easy reference.

Chapter 1 consists of a brief historical commentary on the Mong and their cultural background. This chapter includes their demography and geography, religion, family life, social structure, political organization, economic structure, arts and crafts, language, and education, including the structure of education in Laos, and the Lao education and its impact on the Mong.

Chapter 2 addresses early Mong history. Four theoretical frameworks of the origin of the Mong will be examined. These theories include the Mesopotemian origin, the Ultimate Southern Origin, the China origin, and the Russian origin. Within this context, a discussion of the Mong migration and their interaction with the Chinese through the seventeenth century will be discussed as well.

Chapter 3 provides a historical perspective on French Colonialism, the development of Lao-Franco schools, a discussion of the relationship between the French and the Mong. This chapter addresses the major influences that shaped the Mong society and their education in the years to come. In addition, the chapter covers the impact of World War II on Mong, the Vietnam Conflict (including the US Secret Army in Laos and the Commemoration of the Mong Veterans in the US), the emergence of Christianity in conjunction with the Mong literacy development, a brief history of the Lao Evangelical Church, and the ongoing internal political tripartite conflict within the former Lao government.

Chapter 4 investigates the Mong in transition from the refugee camps in Thailand during their resettlement process in the US and other western countries. This chapter will examine the refugee registration process, the Refugee Act of 1980 (PL 96-212), the Mong resettlement by the national Voluntary Agencies (VOLAGs) and their roles, and the Mong resettlement across the US and their general adjustment difficulties.

Chapter 5 provides a critical analysis of the formal education system in Laos in relation to the system in the US. The discussion entails the numerous social and educational problems that Mong students encounter. Those problems include some of the most challenging contemporary issues that Mong parents and urban American public schools nationwide currently face. Chapter 5 closes with some recommendations to remedy these situations.

Chapter 6 examines the linguistic aspects of the Mong language structure in comparison to English. This chapter offers practical educational information to pre-service and in-service teachers from K-12, specially illustrating the linguistic difficulties that Mong limited English proficient (LEP) students may experience. The focus is centered around issues of language acquisition. This includes a discussion on the characteristics of Mong-speaking students, a comparative discussion of the two Mong regional dialects and English in the areas of phonology, morphology, syntax, and the socio-linguistic aspects. The author will provide some suggestions for classroom teachers and educators on how to deal with Mong limited English proficient (LEP) students to accommodate a smooth transition from Mong to English-only classrooms.

Finally, chapter 7 contains an open letter addressed to the Mong, to Mong students, to the Voluntary Organizations (VOLAGs), to local school officials and to federal and state agencies. Specific recommendations will assist these audiences to cope with the Mong and similar populations in the event that large groups of unfamiliar immigrants arrive in the US unexpectedly. The reader will also benefit from a list of available resources that equip classroom teachers with grade level appropriate reference materials.

Notes

[1] Paoze Thao, Mong Resettlement in the Chicago Area (1978-1987): Educational Implications, Ph.D. Dissertation, Loyola University of Chicago, 1994, p. 183-184.

8 *Introduction*

[2] Office of Refugee Resettlement, *Report to Congress FY 1993: Refugee Resettlement Program* (Washington, DC: US Department of Health and Human Services, Administration of Children and Families, 1993), A2-A3.
[3] Ibid., p.A-3.
[4] Paul Marahail, ed. By Hugo Adolf Bernatzik, *Akha and Miao* (Innesbruck: Kommissionsverlag Wagners'sche Univ., 1947), 7. English Translation: Human Relations Area Files, 1970.
[5] Ibid., 7.
[6] Ibid., 8.
[7] Ibid., 8-9.
[8] George L. Barney and William A. Smalley, "Third Report on Meo (Miao): Orthography and Grammar." Mimeo, 1953.
[9] G.A. Binney, *The Social and Economic Organization of Two White Meo Communities in Thailand* (Washington: Advanced Research Program Agency, 1968).
[10] A.G. Haudricourt, *Problemes de Phologie Diachronique* (Paris, France: Centre National de Recherche Scientifique, 1972).
[11] F.M. Savina, *Abecedaire Meo-Francaise* (Meo-French Primer) (Hanoi: Imprimerie d'Extreme Orient, 1920.
[12] William A. Smalley, "The Problems of Consonants and Tone: Hmong (Meo, Miao)," *Phonemes and Orthography: Language Planning in Ten Minority Languages of Thailand* (Canberra: Australian National University, 1976), 4:85-123.
[13] Cheu Thao and Barbara Robson, *Interim Report on the Mhong Language Council Conference August 12-14, 1982* (Washington, DC: Center for Applied Linguistics, 1982).
[14] Ibid., 1-4.
[15] Dao Yang, *Les Hmong du Laos Face au Developpement* (Vientiane, Laos: Edition Siaosavath, 1975).
[16] Victoria Fromkin and Robert Rodman, *Introduction to Language.* 6th Ed. (Fort Worth, TX: Harcourt Brace College Publishers, 1998), p. 226-227.
[17] Ibid., p. 260-261, 266 and 288.
[18] Thomas Amis Lyman, *Grammar of Mong Njua (Green Miao): A Descriptive Linguistic Study* (Belgium: Published by the Author, 1979).
[19] Lang Xiong; Joua Xiong; and Nao Leng Xiong, *English-Mong-English Dictionary* (Milwaukee, WI: Hetrick Printing, Inc., 1983).
[20] Paoze Thao, Mong Resettlement in the Chicago Area (1978-1987): Educational Implications, Ph.D. Dissertation, Loyola University of Chicago, 1994; and *Kevcai Siv Lug Moob* (Foundations of Mong Language), (Marina: CA: PT Publishing, 1997).
[21] Su Thao, *Ncu Txug Txajntsig Moob I and II* [Special Tribute To Commemorate the Mong I and II], (Video) (Fresno, CA: S.T. Universal Studio, 1996).
[22] David S. North et al., *An Evaluation of the Highland Lao Initiative* (Washington, DC: Office of Refugee Resettlement, US Dept. Of Health and Human Services, 1985), 5.
[23] Ibid., Su Thao, 1996.

Chapter 1

The Mong and Their Cultural Background

Chapter I consists of a brief commentary on the Mong and their cultural background. It includes discussion of demography and geography, religion, family life, social structure, political organization, economic structure, arts and crafts, language, and education. This section describes the culture that the Mong as a people brought with them from Southeast Asia. In many ways, these cultural characteristics clash with the dominant culture in the US creating some problems.

Demography and Geography

It has been difficult to accurately estimate the size of the Mong population since no official census have been conducted. However, the overall Mong population in the world may have reached six millions. This estimate is provided by various sources within between 1974 and 1982, and while these figures may be in some dispute, they remain one of the most reliable sources available. In 1982, 5,030,897 Mong lived in China,[1] 250,000 in Vietnam,[2] 125,000 in Thailand (including Mong refugees), 4,000 in Burma (now Myanmar), 165,000 in the United States, 7,500 in France, 1,100 in French Guyana, 700 in

Canada, 350 in Australia, and 130 in Germany.[3] In 1974, 350,000 Mong lived in Laos.[4] Due to the Vietnam conflict, the Mong population in Laos may have decreased to 200,000 at the present time.

The majority of the Mong are found in the remote mountainous regions in the Southern provinces of China (in Kweichow, Yunnan, Kwangsi, Hunan, Szechwan, Kwangtun, Fukien, Chekiang, and Hupeh),[5] in Northern Vietnam (in Lao Cay, Chopa, Lai Chau, Dien Bien Phu),[6] and in Northern Laos (in Houaphanh, Xieng Khouang, Luang Prabang, and Sayaboury).[7]

Geddes concludes that the Mong in Thailand normally live at an altitude of 3,500 feet to 5,000 feet or more.[8] Reed's findings support this notion that the Mong occupied the mountainous regions of Laos at an altitude of between 3,000 feet to 6,000 feet.[9] A two-fold theory suggests that the Mong reside in higher altitude to preserve Mong cultural solidarity and to sustain their love of independence.

Religion

The Mong were traditionally animists. The American Heritage Dictionary defines animism as "any of various primitive beliefs whereby natural phenomena and things animate and inanimate are held to possess an innate soul."[10] Hackett defines the term as "the belief that all life is produced by a spiritual force, or that all things in nature have souls."[11] However, researchers have not reached a consensus on the elements of animism to date. Based on a study of the religious change among the Mong in San Diego, Scott finds that the traditional Mong religion is comprised of three interrelated elements which are animism, ancestor worship and shamanism.[12] The author contends that animism is a belief system that comprises all three elements or more. It combines the one or two supernatural power, ancestor worship, superstition, spirit (*dlaab*) worship and shamanism.

Traditionally, the supernatural power was referred to *Yawm Saub* (God). Ancestor worship of "good" spirits was used to provide protection to Mong families. Spirits of nature, such as *Ntxwg Nyoog* (Satan) and others *dlaab* (evil spirits or devils), were believed to be able to cause physical and psychological harm to Mong in the form of illness, nightmares, and, to a certain extent, death. Shamanism was viewed as the only means of maintaining communication between the Mong and the evil spiritual world. Mong shamans perform rituals to find out the causes of illness in order to treat the effects. By performing rituals with animal sacrifice, the shamans related the message from evil spirits to the individuals involved and vice versa. There are also times when shamans have to perform exorcism of evil spirits as well. Though standardization in Mong religious practices does not exist, Mong rituals tend to center around the practices that their ancestors have passed onto them. Clan and lineage variations also occur between and within clans because rituals are traditionally handed down from generation to generation within the context of oral tradition.[13]

The Mong also believe in life after death. With proper guidance from Mong musicians who perform the funeral ceremony, the Mong believe the souls of the deceased will return to their ancestors for reincarnation, where their new bodies become new members of the Mong families. This is one aspect in which the Mong differ from the Chinese. The Chinese actually worship their dead ancestors while the Mong do not.[14]

For practical purposes, of the three religious elements, the Mong focus primarily on superstition and spirit worship. In a study on Mong Sudden Unexplained Death Syndrome (SUDS), Bliatout asserts that the Mong religious beliefs are closely interwoven with their beliefs on illness and death. Being extremely fearful of the evil spirits' constant demands for taking their souls, larger animals are constantly needed for sacrifice. The Mong believe that they have only two options: either to fight or to surrender to evil spirits for the sake of their family members' health. Those who surrender to the evil spirits need to fulfill the demands of the evil spirits. Those who fight back against evil spirits have to replace them with a stronger God. This option involves becoming Christians and acceptance of Jesus Christ as their Savior.

Ancestor worship is relied upon from time to time in circumstances where a family member is deceased. Proper guidance necessitates the spirit of the deceased to return to his/her ancestors. To most of the Mong, the term "ancestors" refers to God. With the passage of time, today the Mong tend to remember only two elements, which are shamanism and spirit worship. Instead of turning to worship the Supreme power which is God, the Mong have been psychologically compelled to spiritual worship not by choice, but by fear related to health issues.

Family Life

I will now turn to the traditional structure of the Mong family life. As the basic nurturing institution, the Mong family is the most important unit in Mong society. It consists of all the people living under the authority of a household. This is often referred to as the extended family. One of the most distinctive characteristics of the Mong family is that it is organized strictly in a patrilineal fashion. This means that when a Mong child is born, he/she automatically takes on the father's clan name. However, when a Mong woman gets married, she is detached from her clan and loses all the rights provided to her from her original clan. Though she still has connection with her own family and her clan, she will assume a new identity within her husband's new clan. She will be embraced in the new family and clan, and will enjoy all the privileges and rights that are guaranteed to her under the auspices of her husband and his clan. On a separate but related issue, each member of the Mong family is assigned specific tasks and works diligently to contribute to the welfare of the family: the male breadwinning, the wife housework, children tedious and simple manual labor work, and grandparents childcare and educating the young.

Social Structure

Besides the importance of the concept of family and extended family, the Mong place emphasis on the clan system that originated from a common ancestor. The clanship is considered the basic social and political organization in the Mong society. A Mong at birth automatically takes his/her father's clan name and remains a member for life except for the Mong women who marry and assume new identities in their husbands' clans as discussed previously. However, the origin of the clan remains a mystery. Mong legends refer to the clandestine origin to a child of incest born from a brother and a sister dating back to the Great Flood. Shaped like an egg, the offspring is cut into twelve pieces by its parents. The twelve pieces became the twelve different Mong clans. The traditional Mong consisted of twelve clans that corresponded to their rituals. Mong rituals are related to Mong religion directly. Because there is no standardization in Mong religious practices, religious rituals among the clans vary from clan to clan, and from family to family. This means that only those Mong families considered close relatives share the same rituals. The Mong have an old saying: "*Tug tuag tug tsev tau*" [One cannot die in another person's house]. This means that only close relatives, mainly those who are of the same lineage from the same family, can die in their home. Those who allow other Mong clan members or distant relatives to die in their homes will bring misfortune and even death to their own families and to their own clans. This is why Mong rituals are extremely important for those traditional Mong who still practice animism as part of their religion.

The following describe the original rituals that are constantly referred to by their Mong clan names. These names have some close connections with the geographical areas or regions where the Mong had settled in China. Each of the original twelve clans has their own distinct rituals, (including family rituals with the same ancestors) that correspond to their clan names. The names of the rituals are only written in Mong and cannot be translated into English. For the time being, they only carry meaning for the Mong themselves. The Mong rituals are very interesting and the author encourages further studies in this field. The following are the original twelve Mong clans with the names of their corresponding distinct rituals:

Clan Names	Rituals in Mong
1. *Chang (Chun)*	*Nrig*
2. *Hang*	*Taag*
3. *Her*	*Dluag*
4. *Kue*	*Nkug*
5. *Khang, Phang**	*Pluag*
6. *Lee (Li, Ly), Lor**	*Cai*
7. *Moua (Mua)*	*Zaag*
8. *Song*	*Koo*
9. *Thao (Thor)*	*Dlub*
10. *Vang, Cheng*, Fang*, Vue**	*Vug*
11. *Xiong*	*Mob*
12. *Yang*	*Yawg*

The following historical interpretations discuss the development of the origin of the twelve clans of the Mong and the subsequent branching out of the twelve into the eighteen Mong clans of today. Even though the origin of the clans of the Mong is unknown, a possible explanation may be deducted from historical accounts. During the early Chou Dynasty (1028-257 BC), the Mong appear to have enjoyed a positive relationship with the Chinese. This was evidenced by the Mong's willingness to take on Mandarin clan names. This significant incident of accepting Chinese Mandarin clan names must have taken place during the Chou Dynasty but before Confucius' time, which was around the second century B.C.[15] Savina reported:

> "At the time of Confucius...there were still twelve noble and powerful families."[16]

These twelve noble and powerful families described above could have been the twelve clans of the Mong. A Chinese legend stated that the Mong assisted King Wu, the first king of the Chou Dynasty (1028-257 BC), to fight against the last emperor of the Shang Dynasty. Though history did not mention how King Wu rewarded the Mong, after his victory, King Wu and the Mong may have had intensified their positive relationship. They may have taken an oath to assist each other as brothers in times of need. This relationship was reflected in the Mong's term *"kwvtij"* (brothers). Mong referred to themselves as *"tij"* (older brother) and to the Chinese as *"kwv"* (younger brother). When the two words compounded as *"kwvtij"* (brothers), the relationship between the Mong and the Chinese may have developed to the level of an intimate brotherhood. The term *"kwvtij"* also existed in Chinese Mandarin which means the reverse of the meaning in Mong. In Chinese Mandarin, *"kwv"* means older brother and *"tij"* younger brother.

Another Mong legend states that a Mong went to pay respect to the tomb of his ancestor once a year. The Chinese paid the same respect to the same tomb once a year but at a different time of the year. One year, the Mong and the Chinese came to pay respect to the same tomb at the same time. Then, after a conversation, the Mong and the Chinese found out that they were descendants from the same ancestor. This is why the term "*kwvtij*" meaning [brother], was coined for both Mong and Chinese Mandarin vocabulary.

As time passed, the distance between the Mong and the Chinese became greater. Though history does not disclose such details, the subsequent emperors of the Chou Dynasty may have forgotten the oath taken with the Mong in the old days. The historical record is inconclusive as to the reasons why the Chinese repeatedly tried to eradicate the Mong in China. Quincy indicates that Mandarin scholars were sent to live with the Mong and to learn their ways in order to control them during the late Chou Dynasty.[17]

Another interesting observation concerns the branching out of the Mong clan system from twelve to eighteen clans. This evolution of the clan system may have occurred during the Ming Dynasty (1368-1644). The Ming desired trade with Southeast Asia, and thus needed to annex Yunan to create a passage to Burma (Myanmar). Military zones and administrative districts were created to capture new lands to form the new provinces. Each province was administratively divided into three Prefectures "*Fu*," four sub-prefectures "*Zhou*," and seventy-five cantons "*Zhang-kwang-si*." Local chiefs were employed as "*Tu Si*" (officers) and "*Tu Kwan*" (tax collectors) by all the administrative units under the "Fu" to handle military and civil affairs at the local levels.[18] Quincy asserted that the Lolo tribes were granted *Tu Si* and often appointed Mong as sub-officials to maintain peace among their people.[19] The Mong term "*Kabtoom*" or "*Katong*" was perhaps derived from "Cantons" meaning the chief of Canton. In order to justify to Chinese authority increasing the numbers of *Katong* positions in the Mong tribes, the notion was that "*Tu Si*" appointed one *Katong* per clan. By branching out their clans, the Vang would have been entitled to four *Katongs* under Vang, Cheng, Fang, and Vue; the Khang and the Lee to two; and other clans to one *Katong* per clan.

Political Organization

Traditionally, the Mong had a fairly complex hierarchical political system that reflects the former political system of the Mong kingdom that existed between 400-900 AD. According to Quincy, the Mong political system was "a loose federation of tribal heredity monarchy" that defied absolute power but exhibited certain democratic, participatory, and republican features since the real power was decentralized to the localities. The successor of a Mong monarch was elected by the people among the Mong princes.[20] The Mong monarchy was based on the natural leaders' ability to rule rather than on a continuum of an organized political structure. The entire political and social structure was centered around the monarchy. Due to their illiteracy, when the Mong natural patriarchs died, the monarchy collapsed. Thus, the full scope of the traditional Mong political system has been difficult to determine.

When the Mong migrated from China to Laos in the early nineteenth century, some alterations in their political structure were made under the auspices of the territorial organization of the Royal Laotian government. The following discussions may be helpful to explain that particular political hierarchy and organization.

A typical Mong village was comprised of between six to thirty families that formed a village headed by a *Nai Ban* (headman) who served as the village representative to handle matters for all members in his village. Several villages formed a canton and its chief, *Tasseng* (a district chief) was elected. *Tasseng* was often appointed by the *Chao Muong* (Mayor) on the recommendations of several *Nai Ban*. Another higher layer of civil tribal administrative officials beyond the *Tasseng* was the *Nai Kong* whose authority corresponded to the *Tasseng*. The *Tasseng* was responsible for the coordination of the affairs of several villages under his jurisdiction, to collect taxes, and to enforce the law. *Tasseng* reported directly to the *Chao Muong* (Mayor). Technically, *Nai Kong* was a civil tribal administrative official that was higher in rank than Tasseng and was supposed to be a collection of several district chiefs. Practically, *Nai Kong's* position was more of a "floating" or "at large" position. *Nai Kong* was mainly responsible for recruitment of soldiers for the military. The *Chao Muong* was a collection of several districts and was appointed by the *Chao Khoueng* (provincial chief or equivalent to governor). Seven or eight *Muong* (cities) formed a province headed by *Chao Khoueng* (provincial chief) appointed by the Minister of the Interior and Social Welfare.[21]

Despite these hierarchical layers, the strongest basic unit of the Mong political system remained with the patrilineal clan system at the local level. The members of the same clan refer to one another as clan-brothers or clan-sisters. Due to this clan orientation, the idea of grouping or clustering the members of any clan in one particular area into an enclave or community is typical. The underlying rationale for the Mong enclave is to provide mutual assistance to one another in time of need, such as marriages, celebrations, funerals, and problem resolution. The clan system was considered the integral part of the cornerstone of the Mong authority.

G. Linwood Barney, a missionary to Laos during the 1950's, asserted that the Mong political authority involved the concept of respect for the elders.[22] The Mong placed a high value on older people.

It was customary for young people to pay respect and express gratitude towards the elderly. The elderly had more life experience than the young and thus their views were honored. The hierarchy of respect usually proceeded from the child to the older brothers, parents, grand-parents to *Tug tsawsntug* (the householder), who has the final authority in familial matters. Before a decision was reached a thorough consideration of the best alternatives was assessed. Therefore, a Mong was answerable to his family, his clan, and particularly to the head of the household who maintained peace and harmony within his family, clan members, and members of other clans.

To sum up, the Mong political system was closely tied to its clan system and even today remains strongest at the local level where most of the decisions are carried out.

Economic Structure

As economically self-suffi﹅ient farmers, the traditional Mong grew rice as their main crop in paddy fields in the basin of the Yellow River and the Yangze-kiang River in China. "*Laj aj tebchaws*" (paddy field country) was well known by the Mong for centuries. After the Chinese invasion, the Mong were driven off these fertile lands to the remote mountains. As mountain dwellers, they were forced to survive in a traditional agricultural economy "*Ua-teb*" (farming) at the subsistence level. They grew rice, maize, potatoes, pumpkins, cucumbers, watermelons, and other crops. Adequate food was grown for their families and some extra for sale. The Mong also raised livestock, such as chicken, pigs, cows, ducks, and fish for protein, water buffaloes for the cultivation of land and for farming, and horses for transportation. The Mong brought this agricultural economy with them when they migrated to Laos in the early nineteenth century.

The notion of division of labor was obviously important within the family, between members of the villages, and between villages. This was closely related to social and political patterns. Everyone in the family worked hard throughout the year and took part in the production of crops, such as cultivating the land, planting the crops, weeding, harvesting, and storing food. The Mong firmly believed in the spirit of collective teamwork. Therefore, the notion of free labor exchange has had a long existence within the traditional cultural realm of Mong life.

A few Mong families also grew poppy as a cash crop. Poppy cultivation probably originated in Cyprus around 1500 BC, during the late Bronze Age. Opiates may have been sent to Egypt, Greece, and Rome as a pain killer. Opium was recognized as a pain reliever as early as the fourth century BC.[23] Geddes also indicated that poppy was brought to China about the seventh century BC by Arab traders for medical purposes. However, it was not extensively used in "China and countries to the south" until the eighteenth century.[24] Based on this historical account, an inference could be made that it was the Chinese who probably introduced poppy cultivation to the Mong as a cash crop. Mickey asserted that the chief crop in Kweichow, China was opium.[25] However, not all the Mong were content with poppy cultivation. Kemp reported that the Mong ("Miao") in Kweichow were compelled to plant a certain proportion of poppy when they rented the land from the Chinese and that Mong Christians were persecuted for refusing to do so.[26]

It is assumed that the Mong possibly brought poppy seeds with them when they migrated to Southeast Asia in the early nineteenth century. They grew it mainly as a cash crop to pay their taxes to the French and to supply to the French opium monopoly during their colonial administration in Indochina.[27] Despite the Mong's dissatisfaction and opposition to poppy cultivation, Larteguy, in *La Fabuleuse Aventure du Peuple de l'Opium*, still stigmatized the Mong as the people of opium.[28]

Arts and Crafts

The Mong are very well-known for their arts and crafts, such as the *Paaj Ntaub* (Pan-Dau). Mong women probably first observed the patterns wed in cross stitch embroidery and applique in the design of the Cowrie Shell from the shape of animals and plants in China. These patterns have been incorporated into costume design, such as caps, jackets, baby carrying cloth, aprons, skirts, turbans, bags, men's sashes, flower cloths, quilts, baby carriers, covering for altars and beds, pillow cases, etc. Nowadays, Mong *Paajntaub* (pronounced Pan-dau, meaning arts and crafts) has become one of the most distinctive features of traditional Mong culture. Most of this work has been fully illustrated by the work of Lewis and Lewis' in their book, *Peoples of the Golden Triangle: Six Tribes in Thailand*. Since 1968, they have extensively gathered the arts and crafts from six of the culturally distinct minority groups in Thailand: Karen, Mong, Mien, Lahu, Akha, and Lisu along with over 700 photographs in color. Their work featured one of the most complete documentation of the fascinating colorful Mong clothing and ornamentation exhibited through their arts and crafts.[29]

Language

The Mong language is classified by linguists as a subgroup in the Sino-Tibetan language family of Asia. According to Arlotto, the Mong language is considered one of the pre-Sinitic languages:

Within China itself, among the few remaining pre-Sinitic languages
we have the Miao-Yao family, spoken by scattered remnants of
what once undoubtedly was a widespread and flourishing family.[30]

This means that the Mong had long existed prior to 1300 BC. Kun
Chang indicated that the term "Miao" existed as early as the *Book of
Documents* and the Miao people had been in contact with the Chinese
at least since the Shang-Chou Dynasty.[31]

Mong is a syllabic, tonal, and harmonious language. The
orthography currently used was based on a refinement of the
Romanized Popular Alphabet (RPA) system developed by
missionaries of the Christian and Missionary Alliance (CMA),
Linwood G. Barney (known by the Mong as Thanh Mong) and
William A. Smalley, and a French Catholic Priest, Father Yves
Bertrais (known by the Mong as Txivplig Nyaj Pov) during the early
1950's. The Mong language consists of sixty-three phonemes (nineteen
single consonants, twenty-four double consonantal blends, sixteen
triple consonantal blends, and four quadruple consonantal blends), ten
vowel phonemes (six single vowel phonemes and four diphthongs),
and eight different vocal tone markers. It is predictable that almost all
of the Mong words end with tone markers represented by the letters **b**,
j, **v**, **--**, **s**, **g**, **m**, and **d**. These letters at the end of each Mong lexicon
are tone markers and the tones are not arbitrary. The elements of Mong
language are discussed more in-depth in Chapter 6.

Education

Little is known about Mong education in China during the pre-historic
period up till the eighteenth century. It is the author's assumption that
the first Mong inhabitants in China made their living through a self-
initiated type of informal education system, consisting of small scale
farming, domestic animal keeping, hunting, and trapping. As time
passed, guilds, such as blacksmith, silversmith, craftmaking,
clothesmaking, shamanism, and related customs, and rituals were
developed. These skills then were passed on informally from father to
son, from mother to daughter, and from generation to generation
within the familial context. Gutek referred to the informal aspects of
education as:

> the total cultural context in which persons are born, nurtured, and
> brought to maturity. Through the process of enculturation, they
> acquire the symbolic, linguistic, and value patterns of their
> culture.[32]

History reveals that the Mong had received some formal education
from the Chinese. Between 1801 and 1804, a concerted effort was
made by the Chinese to Sinicize the Mong in Kweichow, China.

Chinese civil authorities forced Mong "children to attend Chinese schools."[33] However, history failed to give us further details on how education of the Mong was conducted.

In Laos, since the seventeenth century, King Setthathirath founded the first official Buddhist schools in Laos.[34] Through this Buddhist influence, pagoda schools were always centered in the village Buddhist temples. Prior to the Communist era (1975), it was a tradition for Lao men to become novice monks to pay gratitude to their parents before starting their own families. Boys and men were required to enter monkhood for two or three weeks to participate in the preservation and the teaching of Buddhism.[35] Monastic education was the sole system to provide education to boys up to the arrival of the French. Curricula included the study of Pali religious texts, orientated primarily to practical needs and full participation in traditional Lao village society; the study of Lao language, religious and domestic ethics, basic law, and manual training in the arts and crafts, and religious fields.[36] The Buddhist monks were considered the best teachers at that time. Only those boys and men who entered monkhood enrolled in the pagoda schools and had the opportunity to further their education through the curricula mentioned above throughout their lives of monkhood. Those who became novice monks for the duration of two to three weeks barely went through the basic teachings of Buddhism. There is no historical evidence suggesting that the Mong participated in the pagoda schools or any of the subsequent schools until the arrival of the French.

During French Colonialism, though the French imported their educational system to Laos, the Mong benefited very little from it. Only a few Mong had the opportunity to attend school. Nao Tou Moua, head of the Moua clan, was the first Mong to send his children to school at a French elementary school in Xieng Khouang in 1935. In addition, two more Mong, Touby and Tou Zeu Lyfoung continued their education and received their baccalaureate certificates from French institutions in Vietnam. Touby Lyfoung became a prominent Mong political figure in Laos during the Neo-colonialist period in the following two decades. He was appointed deputy to the provincial governor in 1946 (known as *Chao Muong Meo* or the Mong Mayor) and in 1960's as advisor to King Sisavang Wattana. Tou Zeu Lyfoung continued his education in France and graduated as the first Mong in Laos with a bachelor's degree.[37]

Yang asserted that the first primary school for Mong was built in Xieng Khouang, Laos in 1939.[38] James Seying, formerly known as Mang Thao, was a former administrative officer with the Office of the Inspector of Primary Education in Xieng Khouang, Laos. Seying recalled that in 1958-1959, four Mong attended and graduated from *l'Ecole Normal* in Vientiane (consisting of Lee Blong, Moua Lia, Lee Beu, and Lee May See) and five from Xieng Khouang Teacher's

Training College (consisting of Siong Je, Tou Lor Lee, Ka Ying Yang, Lee Phia, and Yang Sao). In the 1960's, Mong students increased to 1,500 attending twenty village schools. *Pha Khao* and *Samthong* School districts were instituted in 1962 with the expansion of village primary schools.[39]

By 1969, the numbers of students grew to 10,000 with 450 teachers administered through seven school districts overseen by Moua Lia, the Inspector of Primary Education.[40] Furthermore, Yang indicated that by 1971, 340 Mong attended public and private secondary schools in Vientiane, and thirty-seven studied abroad in various universities: twenty-five in France, four in Canada, four in the United States, one in Australia, one in Italy, one in Japan, and one in the Soviet Union.[41]

Seying further recalled that in 1975, primary education expanded to include nine school districts with 164 schools, 20,000 students (eighteen percent were ethnic Lao and Khamu), thirty third-rank teachers (beginners), twenty second-rank teachers, and 200 temporary seasonal teachers. There were no first-rank teachers in Mong schools. School supplies were made possible by the United States Agency for International Development (USAID).[42]

Structure of Education in Laos

The Development of Lao Education during Post-Colonialism

During the Post-Colonial period between 1947-1975, education in Laos was centralized under the Minister of National Education, Fine Arts, Youth and Sports. The Director General of Education was the key person who oversaw the overall programs. He coordinated the activities of all National Directorates and internal services of the Ministry. Curricula were set by the Directorate of National Education. Elementary schooling was traditionally financed by the local communities. The subjects taught in elementary schools corresponded closely with the earlier period. Subjects included ethics and civics, history, geography, arithmetic, drawing or manual work, singing, and physical culture.[43]

Secondary education in Laos was very limited but selective. Only five high schools were established since 1949 that provided three-year lower secondary certificates in Laos. When students completed their third year, they continued their fourth year at *Lycee Pavie* in Vientiane, Laos. Curricula in the secondary level included ethics and civics, French, Lao, English, history, geography, French literature, mathematics, physical culture, drawing, music, and manual work. Instruction was in the French language and was similar to the French modern and classical *lycee*. It was reported that not more than 200 students enrolled in upper secondary levels. The numbers of students were increased to 652 in 1955 and 2,396 in 1959, a decade later.[44] A different source also reported that student enrollment in the teacher preparation program needed to be increased by 100 in 1955.[45]

The most important event relating to the development of national education in Laos was the Royal Ordinance of Educational Reform of 1962. It recast the whole educational system by incorporating the Buddhist temple schools and emphasizing vocational training in the kingdom. The Act provided a charter for regulating the system of education in Laos to meet the country's needs. This change influenced the structure, content and methods, administrative cadres and teaching personnel.[46] (See Table 1. - Structure of Education in Laos).

The ordinance divided elementary education into two cycles: elementary and the second primary. The elementary cycle was offered at the village level emphasizing Lao as the language of instruction; whereas the second primary cycle was given at a district central school called "*Groupe Scolaire.*" French language instruction began from this level. A *groupe scolaire* usually had all six grades. It combined the two cycles of primary education. G. Provo indicated that student enrollment was increased to 1,525 in 1966, and to 1,769 in 1967-1968.[47] Outsama reported that a total of 3,171 elementary schools were opened to accommodate 216,687 students between 1970-1971.[48] This expansion of education could not have been accomplished without the accelerated teachers training program of *l'Ecole Normal de Vientiane* (later became *l'Ecole Superieure de Pedagogie*). To meet the needs of educational expansion, with aid from USAID, students were asked to sign promissory notes that they would teach for the government. Stipends and scholarships were awarded to stimulate Lao students to become teachers. No prior statistics on the budget for education was available. However, education was funded through the national budget and constituted nearly twelve percent (12%) of all expenditures. In 1973-1974, about 2 billion kips (about $3,300) were allocated for education.

After completing elementary schools, students could go on to the general stream, teacher's training, technical and vocational education in secondary schools. The General stream included four years of first cycle and three years of second cycle. Students passing this stream would move on to universities and other institutions of higher education.

The accelerated teacher's training consisted of two years after elementary. However, the regular stream of teacher training in Laos included four years in the first cycle and three years in the second cycle.

Technical and vocational education consisted of two cycles: four years for the first cycle and three for the second cycle. Three areas of training were available: agriculture and animal husbandry, industry and construction and handicrafts, and commerce and administration.

Table 1. Structure of Education in Laos: Schooling Under the Ministry of Education, Fine Arts, Youth and Sports

(Standard Age)	3	4	5	6	7	8	9	10	11	12	13	14	15	16	17	18	19
Pre-School	●	●	●														
Primary Education — General Stream Grades (1st Cycle)(2nd Cycle)				1	2	3	4	5									
Secondary Education — General Stream (6 7 8 9 10 11 12 13)									6	7	8	9	10	11	12	13	
Technical and Vocational Education											7	8	9	10	11	12	1
School of Laotian Aart											7	8	9	10			
Home Economics											1	2					
Teacher Training											1	2	3	4	5	6	7
Accelerated Training											1	2					
College of Education (E.S.P.)														1	2	3	4
School of Rural Handicrafts											7	8					
Royal School of Medicine (First Cycle 11 12 13; Second Cycle 1 2 3 4 5 6 —)															11	12	13
Royal Institute of Law & Administration (First Cycle 11 12 13; Second Cycle 1 2 3)															11	12	13
Dance and Music School (Natasinh) (First Cycle 4 5 6 1 2 3; Second Cycle 1 2)							4	5	6	1	2	3					
Higher Education — Universities and other institutions																	●

Source: Adapted from Kao Outsama, "Educational Administration in Laos," *Bulletin of the UNESCO Regional Office of Education in Asia.No. 15. Administration of Education in the Asian Region* (Bangkok, Thailand: UNESC), 1974), p. 118.

Students could go on to four years of lower secondary school at the School of Laotian Arts, two years at the School of Rural Handicrafts, three years in the first cycle and two years at the Dance and Music School (*Natasinh*), three years in the second cycle in the Royal School of Medicine, three years in the second cycle at the Royal Institute of Law and Administration or two years in Home economics.

For higher education, three disciplines were offered within the framework of Sisavangvong University promulgated by the Royal Decree 164 of June 30, 1958: medical training provided by the Royal School of Medicine, teacher training by *l'Ecole Superieure de Pedagogie*, and law by the Royal Institute of Law and Administration.[49]

Lao Education and Its Impact on the Mong

In terms of Mong education, Yang asserted that the first primary school for Mong was built in Xieng Khouang, Laos in 1939. There was no statistical report on the Mong students who enrolled in that school in that year. However, in the 1960's, Mong students increased to 1,500 attending twenty village schools. By 1969, the numbers of Mong students grew to 10,000 with 450 teachers administered through seven school districts overseen by Moua Lia, the Inspector of Primary Education. By 1971, 340 Mong attended public and private secondary schools in Vientiane, Laos, and 37 studied abroad in various universities in foreign countries: twenty-five in France, four in Canada, four in the United States, one in Australia, one in Italy, one in Japan, and one in the Soviet Union.[50]

Another reliable source on the impact of Lao education on Mong was obtained from James Seying. Formerly known as Mang Thao, he was a former administrative officer with the Office of Inspector of Primary Education in Xieng Khouang, Laos during the Post-Colonialism period (1947-1975). Seying recalled that, in 1958-1959, there were only four Mong who graduated from l'Ecole Normal in Vientiane, Laos (Lee Blong, Moua Lia, Lee Beu, and Lee May See) and five from Xieng Khouang Teacher's Training College (Siong Je, Tou Lor Lee, Ka Ying Yang, Lee Phia, and Yang Sao). Then, in 1962, only two school districts were instituted. They were *Pha Khao* and *Samthong* School Districts with the expansion of village primary schools. In 1975, primary education for Mong expanded to include nine school districts with 164 schools, 20,000 students (eighteen percent were ethnic Lao and Khamu and eighty-two percent Mong), thirty third-rank teachers (beginners), twenty second-rank teachers, and 200 temporary seasonal teachers. There were no first-rank Mong teachers in Mong schools. School supplies were made possible by USAID.[51]

Summary

This chapter briefly examined the demography and geography where the Mong lived, religion, family life, the traditional social structure, political organization, economic structure, arts and crafts, language, education, and the structure of education in Laos that have impacted the Mong in the United States today. The Lao traditional school system consisted mainly of the pagoda schools influenced by Hindu-Buddhist principles until the arrival of the French. During the colonization, the French imported their educational system which was highly centralized and selective for implementation in Laos. Curricula and instruction were in the French language until 1975 except for the elementary level dictated by the Royal Decree of 1962.

Chapter 2 will investigate Mong early political history that was recorded by Western researchers and Chinese intellectuals, with commentary through the eyes of the author.

Notes

[1] Chij Tsaj, *Hmoob Nyob Pa Tawg Teb* (The Mong in Wenshan). (Guyane France: Association Communaute Hmong. n.d.), 17.

[2] Dao Yang, *Les Hmong du Laos Face au Developpement* (Vientiane, Laos: Edition Siaosavath, 1975), 26-28.

[3] Xeev Nruag Xyooj, "Txooj Moob huv Nplaj Teb" (The Mong in the World), *Txooj Moob*, Vol. 4 (Winfield, Illinois: Mong Volunteer Literacy, Inc., May 1989), 8-12.

[4] W.E. Garrett, "The Hmong of Laos: No Place to Run," *National Geographic*, Vol. 145, No. 1 (Washington, DC: National Geographic Society, January 1974), 80.

[5] W.R. Geddes, *Migrants of the Mountains: The Cultural Ecology of the Blue Miao (Hmong Njua) of Thailand* (Oxford: Clarendon Press, 1976), 25.

[6] Jean Mottin, *The History of the Hmong (Meo)* (Bangkok, Thailand: Odeon Store, Ltd., 1980), 42.

[7] Ibid., Yang, 30.

[8] Ibid., Geddes, 38.

[9] Tipawan Truong-Quang Reed, "The Hmong Highlanders and the Lao Lowlander" (Chicago, Illinois: Governor's Information for Asian Assistance, May 1978), 4-7.

[10] The *American Heritage Dictionary*, (U.S.A.: Houghton Mifflin Company, 1982), 111.

[11] Alice Payne Hackett, *Websters NewWorld Dictionary* (U.S.A. Warner Books, 1984), 23.

[12] George M. Scott, "A New Year in a New Land: Religious Change among the Lao Hmong Refugees in San Diego," *The Hmong in the West*. ed. (Minneapolis: University of Minnesota, 1982), 65.

[13] Bruce Thowpaow Bliatout, *Hmong Sudden Unexpected Nocturnal Death Syndrome: A Cultural Study* (Portland, Oregon: Sparkle Publishing Enterprises, 1982), 8-9.
[14] Center for Applied Linguistics, *The Peoples and Cultures of Cambodia, Laos, and Vietnam* (Washington, D.C.: Center for Applied for Linguistics, 1981), 45.
[15] Ruth Hanhoe, *Contemporary Chinese Education* (Armonk, N.Y.: M.E. Sharpe, Inc., 1984), 29.
[16] F.M. Savina, *Histoire des* Miao (Paris: Societe des Mission Etrangeres, 1924), 131.
[17] Keith Quincy, *Hmong: History of a People* (Cheney, Washington: Eastern Washington University Press, 1988), 34.
[18] Mottin, 20-21.
[19] Quincy, 44.
[20] Ibid., 38.
[21] T.D. Roberts et al, *Area Handbook for Laos* (Washington, DC: U.S. Government Printing Office, 1967), 163-164.
[22] G. Linwood Barney, "The Hmong of Northern Laos," (Arlington, VA: National Clearinghouse, Center for Applied Linguistics, General Information #16, n.d.), 28-29.
[23] Peter T. White, "The Poppy", *National Geographic*, Vol. 16, No. 2 (Washington, D.C.: National Geographic Society, February 1985), 114.
[24] Geddes, 201-202.
[25] P.M. Mickey, *The Cowrie Shell Miao of Kweichow* (Cambridge: Peabody Museum of American Archaeology, 1947), 5.
[26] E.G. Kemp, *The Highways and Byways of Kweichow Journal of the Royal Asiatic Society*, North China Branch. Vol. 52), 166 in W. R. Geddes, *Migrants of the Mountains: The Cultural Ecology of the Blue Miao(Hmong Njua) of Thailand* (Oxford: Clarendon Press, 1976), 166.
[27] Quincy, 108-111.
[28] Jean Larteguy, *La Fabuleuse Aventure du Peuple de l'Opium* (Paris: Presses de la Cite, 1979).
[29] Paul Lewis and Elaine Lewis, *Peoples of the Golden Triangle: Six Tribes in Thailand* (London: Thames and Hudson, Ltd., 1984), 100-133.
[30] Anthony Arlotto, *Introduction to Historical Linguistics* (U.S.A.: University Press of America, Inc., 1972), 52.
[31] Kun Chang, *The Reconstruction of Proto-Miao-Yao Tones* BIHP (Berkeley: University of California and Academia Sinica, 1972), 542.
[32] Gerald L. Gutek, *A History of the Western Educational Experience* (Prospect Heights, Illinois: Waveland Press, Inc., 1972), 9.
[33] Quincy, 50.
[34] T.D. Roberts, et al. *Area Handbook for Laos* (Washington, D.C.: U.S. Government Printing Office, 1967), 128-129.
[35] Center for Applied for Linguistics, *The Peoples and Cultures of Cambodia, Laos, and Vietnam* (Washington, D.C.: Center for Applied for Linguistics, 1981), 31.
[36] Human Relations Area Files, 78-79.
[37] Ibid., 131-146.
[38] Yang, 1975, 2:134-136

[39]Letter to author by James Seying, Indianapolis, Indiana, 28 December, 1992.

[40]Ibid., Seying, 28 December, 1992.

[41]Yang, 2:134-136.

[42] Seying, 28 December 1992.

[43] Kao Outsama, "Educational Administration in Laos", *Bulletin of the UNESCO Regional Office for Education in Asia, No. 15, Administration of Education in the Asian Region* (Bangkok: UNESCO, 1974), 115-128.

[44] Human Relations Area Files, 81-84.

[45]G. Provo, *Laos: Programmes et Manuels Scolaires, UNESCO, No. de serie: 1255/BMS.RD/EDM*, (Paris: UNESCO, 1969), 15-16.

[46]Royal Ordinance of 1962, No. 648.

[47]Provo, 15-16.

[48]Outsama, 120-121.

[49] Regional Institute of Higher Education and Development, *Proceedings of the Workshop Held in Singapore 26-29 July 1971*, Singapore, September 1971, 37.

[50]Yang, 1975, 2:134-136.

[51]Seying, 28 December 1992.

Chapter 2

Early Mong History

This chapter provides four theoretical frameworks about the origin of the Mong and their earlier history that interfaced with the Chinese for centuries. Commentaries were made about early Mong history until the Mong migrated to Laos in the eighteenth and nineteenth century.

Origin of the Mong

The Mong as a people have a history of over five thousand years. Having no writing system of their own, their early history was recorded by Western and Chinese scholars. Though Webster indicated that there are two major theoretical views that have been offered to explain the origins of the Mong:[1] the theory of Mesopotemian origin proposed by Savina and the theory of ultimate southern origin proposed by Eickstedt, two additional theories of the Mong origin also emerged - the theory of China origin and the theory of Russian origin. A chronology of Mong history is provided for reference (see Table 2).

Table 2. Chronology of Mong History: Origin of the Mong

Savina: Theory of Mesopotemian Origin	Eickstedt: Theory of Ultimate Southern Origin
Dated back to the Confusion of language in Ta Soa	
Originated from the Pamir in Central Asia	
Belonged to a Subgroup of the Turanians (a Caucasoid people)	
(Were) forced out by the Aryans	
Migrated through Turkestan, Russia, Siberia, Mongolia, Manchuria, Honan, Tibet, the Yellow River	
2497 BC: Tseu-You led the Miao in attach on encroaching Chinese Hoang-Ti (Later the Yellow Emperor)	2400 BC: San Miao at San Wei were exterminated by Emperor Yao & Chun. San Miao were forced out.
206 BC – 220 AD: Mong were forced out to Kansu as a political buffer by Chou Dynasty	
618 AD: Tang Dynasty reconquered Mong territories	
907 AD: Sung Dynasty and Ngao Shing (Mong Princess)	
1360-1644: Ming Dynasty	
1644-1911: Manchu Dynasty	
1810-1820: Mong migrated to Laos by way of Vietnam, Myanmar, and Thailand	
1884: Treaty of Tien Tshin between France and China	
1917-1922: The Mad War [Rog Phimbab] led by Pa Chay against the French	
1941-1945: World War II (known to the Mong as Rog Yivpoos – the "Japanese War"	
1946—The Beginning of the "Cold War"	
1963-1975: The Vietnam War and the U.S. Secret Army in Laos	
1975: Mong Refugees moved to Thailand	
1976 to Present: Mong refugees came to the Western countries: USA, Cuba, France, Germany, French Guiana, Canada and Australia	

1. The Theory of Mesopotemian Origin

The first view was introduced by Savina, a French Catholic missionary sent by the Society for Foreign Missions in Paris to spread the Gospel to the Mong in Laos and in Tonkin in the early 1900's. Based on his interpretation of Mong legends, the Mong came from the Pamir area in Central Asia before migrating to other parts of China.[2] Quincy indicated that: "this region encompasses present day Iraq and Syria."[3] After years of research, Savina concluded that the ancestors of the Mong were a subgroup of the Turanians, a Caucasoid people who were forced out by the Aryans. No one knows the prehistoric migration of the Mong except through their legends. After the confusion of languages according to the Bible, the Mong ancestors headed toward a region, "*Taj xuabzeb haav suabpuam*" (sandy region) referred to as "*Ta Soa*" by Savina, then "toward another region behind the back of China." The Mong continued their course of migration from central Asia proceeding through Turkestan, Russia, Siberia, Mongolia, Manchuria, Honan, Tibet, and then the plains of the Yellow River.[4] This oral history remains the only remnants of the Mong from antiquity to Hoang-ti or the Yellow Emperor, which was 2497 BC.[5] Whether the Mong were a subgroup of the Turanians, a Caucasoid race, whose origin was from Mesopotamia, the quest remains inconclusive (see Table 3 – Theories of Mong Origin and Migration).

2. The Theory of Ultimate Southern Origin

Eickstedt, another researcher and an expert on Mong, introduced a second theory proposing the theory of Ultimate Southern Origin. To him, the term "Miao" was derived from the "San-Miao," which is mentioned in the oldest literature in the Sung Period.[6] Mottin explained that the Chinese writings actually referred to the "Sam-Miao" or the "3 Miao."[7] Eickstedt referred to the oldest part of a book called *Schu-djing* which said that "the mythical Emperor Chun forced the San-Meau (spellings of Sam-Meau or San-Meau are inconsistent) to hide away in San-Wei." Father Amiot, a French priest who was in China between 1776 and 1791, wrote that: "In the following year 2282 BC, Chun threw the San-Meau (referring to the San-Miao) back to San-Wei..."[8] (See Table 3. Theories of Mong Origin and Their Migration). Quincy identified the ancient San-Wei as a mountainous area in Southern Kansu[9] (a Chinese province in the southwest of Mongolia).

The view on the original location of the Mong was supported by Graham and Linh Yeuh-Hwa. Based on the Miao folklore, Graham affirmed that the traditions of the Chuan Miao in Szechuan pointed to their former residence in a hot climatic region in the South probably

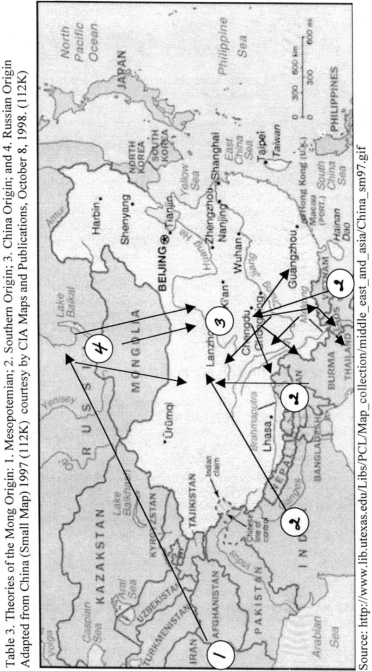

Table 3. Theories of the Mong Origin: 1. Mesopotemian; 2. Southern Origin; 3. China Origin; and 4. Russian Origin
Adapted from China (Small Map) 1997 (112K) courtesy by CIA Maps and Publications, October 8, 1998. (112K)

Source: http://www.lib.utexas.edu/Libs/PCL/Map_collection/middle_east_and_asia/China_sm97.gif

either from India, Burma, or Tonkin prior to migrating into China as far north as the Yellow River.[10] Linh Yeuh-Hwa also spoke of the existence of the San-Miao in a different location from Quincy. This location is located between today Dongtin Lake (in Hunan province) and Payang Lake (in Jiangxi). Linh Yeuh-Hwa asserted that:

> In the late twenty-fourth century BC, the "San-Miao" established a state between lakes Tung-Ting (in Hunan) and P'eng-li (Poyang in northwestern Kiangsi) at San-Wei that required Emperor Yao and Emperor Shun (Choun by Savina) to exterminate them and killed their king.[11]

The theory of Ultimate Southern Origin of the Mong proposed by Eickstedt is also supported by Father LaRocca although he was not aware of its existence during his research. According to LaRocca, after five years of investigated research with a joint cooperative effort from the Chinese authority of the region in Yunnan province, he along with Chu Yongyuan Wu launched a one-month expedition from June 10 to July 1996 to exact and validate his research on the original homeland of the Mong in China. Father LaRocca believes that the Mong originally came from an area referred to as *Li Hu Yen Chi Guen* (meaning "red energy," "red wind," or "red water." This area is situated close to Lancang River, northwest of Langping and Dali in Yunnan, China, which is below Tibet, close to Burma border (East Longitude: 99 degrees 06 minutes and North Latitude: 23 degrees 33 minutes). This entire region is naturally fed from underground thermal springs due to fault lines in the earth. *Li Hu Yen Chi Guen*, one of the thirty-six lakes in the region, is the most powerful and still provides sufficient power for the agriculture in that area. Father LaRocca made a formation declaration of this location as the origin of the "Miaozu" to the Chinese government.[12] Compared to the more original inland location suggested by Linh Yeuh-Hwa, this area is located in the West of the Yunnan province near Burma border.

3. The Theory of China Origin

Though the two previous views existed, most experts on Mong, such as Motin, Bernatzik, Graham, Linh Yeuh-Wah and Geddes collectively agreed that the Mong were in China before the Chinese because it was the Chinese who mentioned the Mong in their history under "Miao." The Mong already occupied the basin of the Yellow River about the twenty-seventh century BC. Due to the rapid expansion of the Chinese, Tseu-You led the Miao attack on the Chinese.[13] Huang-yuan (later Hoang-ti or the Yellow Emperor) defeated the Mong. It is safe to assume that the Chinese had little influence over the Mong during this semi-prehistoric period since Tseu-you's name did not carry a Mandarin clan name as today's Mong do. Geddes estimated that the Mong "were driven off the fertile plains of both the Yellow River and the Yang-tse River some time between 2700-2300 BC.[14] (See Table 3. Theories of Mong Origin and Migration).

4. The Theory of Russian Origin

The Theory of Russian Origin evolved from the work of Lartéguy who researched the Mong in Southeast Asia in the 1950s and re-encountered them again in his hometown Aigoual, France in 1978. He asserted that the Mong had already occupied the vast Siberian plain around Lake Baikal. This area is directly located in Russia North of Mongolia around Lake Baikal area.[15] (See Table 3. Theories of Mong Origin and Migration).

To sum this section, based on all of the research, inlcuding Mong legends and all the documentation available in print, the author concurs with those experts that who agreed that the original homeland of the Mong covers the entire fertile area between the basin of the Yellow River to the basin of the Yang-tse Kiang River referred to the Mong as "*Laj As Tebchaws*" (The Paddy Country). After the Han (Chinese) occupation of the Mong homeland between 2700-2300 BC, the Mong began to migrate from the basins of the Yellow River and the Yang-tse Kiang River to every direction in China.

Mong's Interaction with the Chinese

Since the Hoang-ti era (2497 BC) to the nineteenth century, Mong history was mentioned in part by Chinese whenever there were sedition and revolts by the Mong against the Chinese. History tells us that the Chinese had made many attempts to completely Sinicize the Mong into Chinese culture; whereas the Mong opposed assimilation and full integration. Therefore, various stratagems had been employed to maintain control of the Mong. The following paragraphs exemplify those attempts.

Shang Dynasty (2497 BC.)

Following Tseu-you's (the Mong leader) attack on encroaching Chinese, Hoang-ti (later known as the Yellow Emperor) of the Shang Dynasty reorganized the Mong into the eight-family system, implemented a policy of forced migration to those settlements, and coerced them to abandon their traditional lifestyle from traditional semi-nomadic farmers to sedentary peasants.[16] This particular system became a prominent element of feudalism in ancient China. Though Quincy did not specify what the eight constituents were, the author believes that the Mong may have been divided then into these eight family groups still referred to today: *Moob Sib, Moob Dlub* (Black Mong), *Moob Dlaaj, Moob Suav Faaj, Moob Ncuav Pa, Moob Yob Tshuab, Moob Quasnpaab* (Flowery Mong), and *Moob Lab Haus,* according to the colors of their costumes. These were not linguistic divisions.

Chou Dynasty (1028 - 257 BC)

The Chou Dynasty attempted to banish the Mong. History revealed that during the Chou Dynasty (1028 - 257 BC), the Mong were sent to Southern Kansu to be used as a political buffer in an unsecured location. This particular location was controlled by a group of fierce mountain people led by a chief called "The White Wolf." In addition, Mandarin scholars were sent to learn the Mong's ways to govern the Mong.[17] The Chou Dynasty employed various strategies such as "the tried and true course of material rewards oppression and an extermination campaign policy towards the Mong."[18]

The First Centuries of Chinese History

During the first centuries of Chinese History, the Mong continued their resistance against the Chinese in the basin of the Yellow River and the Hoai (Hwai) despite their losses. The Mong failed to recognize the Chinese Emperors Yao, Choun, and U the Great. A group of Mong was forced to the bend of the Yellow River near Chen-Si and Kansu and the other to the Blue River towards the lakes Tong-T'ieng (Tung Ting in Hunan) and Pouo-Yang (Poyang in northwestern Kiang-si).[19] An old Mong saying was closely related to the Yellow River: "*Tsi pum dlej dlaag sab tsi nqeg*" (If you don't see the Yellow River, you don't believe it).[20] This saying reflected that the Mong must have attempted to cross the Yellow River many times in history but in vain. It implies that warning a person who disbelieves in something is worthless if s/he does not actually see it.

Han Dynasty (206 BC - 220 AD)

Between 206 BC and 220 AD, the Han Dynasty directed a "southern pacification policy" posing serious threats to the Mong by sending military expeditions to quell Mong uprisings.[21]

Tang Dynasty (618 AD)

In 618, the Tang Dynasty launched a campaign to reconquer all territories previously lost to the Mong and brought a great deal of Mong territory under Chinese administrative control.[22]

Sung Dynasty (907 AD)

The most inhumane policy against the Mong occurred during the Sung Dynasty in 907 when various political gimmicks were laid against the Mong. This trickery included the proposed fake marriage of Mong princess, *Ngao Shing*, to a Chinese prince next in line for the throne. The Sung imposed a policy of fight or flight on the Mong. The policy required Mong to wear different clothes of different colors for the purpose of disintegrating unity among the Mong.[23]

Ming Dynasty (1368-1644)

As time went by, Chinese oppression against the Mong during the Ming Dynasty gradually heightened. The Ming Dynasty (1368-1644) continued to capture and to slaughter over forty thousand Mong up till the sixteenth century. Fearing the constant Mong uprising against the Chinese, the "Mong Wall" on the Hunan-Kweichow border was built to prohibit Mong to trade with the Chinese.[24]

Manchu Dynasty (1644-1911)

The Manchu Dynasty (1644-1911) imposed heavy taxes on the Mong to a point of inability to pay, forced Mong children to attend Chinese schools, prohibited Mong traditional celebrations, forced marriage with Mong women, slaughtered Mong indiscriminately, used them as scapegoats for other rebellions, and the worst of all, legalized Chinese prejudice against the Mong by prohibiting the use of Mong language, and urged local officials to suppress the wearing of Mong costumes.[25]

Mong Migration to Laos (1810-1820)

According to Savina, it was the Mong group from the basin of the Hoai who sprawled through Hupeh, Kiang-Si, and Hunan, the Blue River from the basin of the West River. They continued their journey to the northeast as far as Kweichow where the Chinese could not reach them. Savina thought that Kweichow was the base of the Mong concentration where they used to migrate to other provinces such as Kiangsi, in the south to Kwangtung, in the north to Szechwan, and in the west to Yunan.[26] Mottin estimated that the Mong arrived in Laos around 1810-1820 by way of Vietnam.[27]

Summary

The Mong as a people have a history of more than 5,000 years. This chapter attempted to answer two questions - who are the Mong? and where did they come from? by examining their historical background. Having no writing system of their own, early Mong history was recorded in part by Westerners and by Chinese. Four major theoretical views relative to the origins of the Mong were examined. Savina concluded that the Mong were a subgroup of the Turanians, a Caucasoid race, whose origin was from the Pamir area in Mesopotamia. Eickstedt argued that the Mong originated from either India, Burma, or Tonkin. Other collective researchers agreed that the Mong originated from China and Larteguy concluded that the Mong were from Russia. What happened to the Mong when they migrated to Laos in the eighteenth and nineteenth century? What were the major trends that shaped and changed Mong society? These questions will be explored in Chapter 3.

Notes

[1] Leila Webster, "Journey of the Miao," Unpublished paper, 3 December 1978, 5-6.
[2] F.M. Savina, *Histoire des Miao* (Paris: Societe des Missions Etrangeres, 1924), 115.
[3] Keith Quincy, *Hmong: History of a People* (Cheney, Washington: Eastern Washington University Press, 1988), 20.
[4] Savina, 115-123.
[5] Ibid., 115.
[6] E., Frhr. Eickstedt, v. III, "Herkunft und Ausschen de Meau-Stamme in Westchina", Bushchon-Fest scehrift 1943 in Hugo Bernatzik, *Akha and Miao* (New Haven: Human Relations Area Files, Inc. 1970), 6.
[7] J. Mottin, *The History of the Hmong (Meo)* (Bangkok: Odeon Store, Ltd., 1980), 16.
[8] P. I., Amiot, Memoires concernant l'histoire les sciences les arts, les moeurs, les usages e.c. des Chinois" (Bd. 1-15 Paris 1776-1791, bd. 16 Paris
[9] Quincy, 34.
[10] D.C. Graham, "The Customs of the Ch'uan Miao", Journal of the West China Border Research Society, Vol. 9, 1937, pp. 18-20 in W.R. Geddes, Migrants of the Mountains: The Cultural Ecology of the Blue Miao (Hmong Njua) of Thailand (Oxford: Clarendon Press, 1976), 6.
[11] Linh Yeuh-Hwa, "The Miao-Man Peoples of Kwei-chow", *Harvard Journal of Asiatic Studies*, Vol. 5, 1940. This gives a translation of the Miao-Man Section of the Ch'ieng-man Chin-fang chi-lueh written by Lo Jan

Tien in 1847. in W.R. Geddes, "The Originals of the Miao People," *Migrants of the Mountains: The Cultural Ecology of the Blue Miao (Hmong Njua) of Thailand* (Oxford: Clarendon Press, 1976), 4-5.
[12]Interview with Father Jack LaRocca (D. Min), President of Ascent Foundation, San Jose, California, 12 & 19 January 1999; Jack LaRocca, "Miaozu Odyssey: The Searching for Li-Hu-Yen-Chi-Guen, The Hmong Homeland" Daily Journals in an attempt to discover and Explorate the Hmong origin. June 7, 1996 to July 7, 1996, pp. 7-9, 17-19, 21, 45, & 89; and Chu Yongyuan Wu, "In Search of Hmong Origins," *Xuv Ywj Pheej Moob/Hmong Free Press*, Minneapolis, Minnesota. August 1996: 9-10.
[13] Savina, viii.
[14] Geddes, 5.
[15] Jean Lartéguy, La Fabuleuse Aventure du Peuple de l'Opium (Paris, France: Presses de la Cité, 1979), p. 49.
[16] Quincy, 32.
[17] Ibid., 32.
[18] Ibid., 32.
[19] Savina, vii-viii.
[20] Phaj Thoj, *Paaj Lug Moob* {Mong Parables] (Iowa City, Iowa: Published by the Author, 1982), 23.
[21] Quincy., 26.
[22] Ibid, 41.
[23] Ibid, 42-43.
[24] Ibid.,44-46.
[25] Ibid., 29-52.
[26] Savina, iii.
[27] Mottin, 47.

Chapter 3

Impact of Colonialism and War

As part of their struggle for survival, the Mong continued their migration south of China reaching the northern parts of Vietnam, Laos, and Thailand around 1810-1820.[1] In Chapter 3, the major events that shaped and changed Mong society will be examined. These events consisted of French colonialism, World War II, Vietnam War, Christianity and Mong literacy development, and the internal tripartite conflict.

French Colonialism (1892-1947)

Development of Franco-Lao Schools

One of the first major influences that shaped Mong society in the late nineteenth and early twentieth century was the development of Franco-Lao Schools. To understand the impact of French colonialism on the Laotian Educational system, it is necessary to first examine the pre-colonial period. Laos was historically descended from the independent Kingdom of *Lan Xang* (the land of a million elephants) established in Luang Prabang in the mid-fourteenth century. The kingdom reached its political climax by the seventeenth century by controlling sections of China (Yunnan, of the southern Shan states) and large stretches of the present northeastern Thailand.[2]

Two centuries later, the Kingdom of Lan Xang was troubled by external factors such as periodic wars and invasions by the Vietnamese, Thai, and Burmese. It was also disturbed by the internal division of the Kingdom into three separate territories – Vientiane, Luang Prabang, and Champassak -- in 1698 and 1707 AD.[3] As a matter of fact, all three separate territories became present-day Laos.

Religiously, Laos has been influenced by Hindu Buddhism for a long time. According to history, during the third century BC, King Asoka of India was converted to Buddhist. As a Buddhist, he conquered most of the subcontinent by imposing an overlay of Buddhism upon the traditional Brahmanism. Monk Mahinda, King Asoka's emissary, went to Ceylon and converted the Singhalese. Then, the Singhalese brought Buddhism eastward to Burma (Myanmar), Cambodia, Thailand, and Laos. However, it is still unclear as to exactly when Buddhism was introduced to Laos. Thereafter, Buddhism remained the predominant religion in Southeast Asia. Archaeologists found remnants of carved statues of Buddha in Laos dating back to the twelfth century AD. According to the *History of Laos*, in 1356 AD, an official Khmer mission presented Pra Bang Buddha, a Singhalese carving, to the king of Laos. Perhaps the Khmers brought Theravada Buddhism (Lesser Vehicle) to Laos because the first Buddhist pagoda compound "*Wat Keo*" was built in the same year.[4]

However, Buddhism did not flourish until the seventeenth century when King Setthathirath proclaimed Laos a holy Center of Theravada Buddhism. Theravada Buddhism is the doctrine of a Lesser Vehicle that stresses the historical figure of Buddha (the "eternal" guide), Dharma - the teaching of Buddha centering on Karma, and the centrality of the monk's lifestyle and practice (meditation). King Setthathirath founded the first official Buddhist schools in Laos.[5] Through this Hindu-Buddhist influence, pagoda schools together with the Buddhist temples have always been the center of Lao villages. In fact, monastic education was the sole system to provide education to Laotian boys up to the arrival of the French described in greater detail in Chapter 1.

At the turn of the eighteenth century, several western countries began to establish colonial empires in Asia and Africa. As part of this imperialistic trend, France sought colonies in Southeast Asia. By 1893, France conquered Vietnam and Cambodia, occupied the left bank of the Mekong river, and forced Thailand to recognize the Mekong as a natural boundary between Laos and Thailand. Through a series of negotiations with His Majesty King Oun Kham of Luang Prabang, Vice Consul Auguste Pavie[6] convinced the royal court to submit to French protectorate.[7] By conceding to this protectorate, Laos was colonized by the French. The French made no effort to revive the former royal families of Vientiane and Champassak but retained King Oun Kham of Luang Prabang (his royal title).[8] To facilitate this transition, the French imported their entire structure of administration for implementation in Laos. This system was in place in Laos for over fifty years from 1892 to 1947.

As part of the French Indochina, the French were very much in need of bilingual interpreters and functionaries in Laos who had some exposure to western culture to carry out their functions. Between 1902 and 1905, they founded two Franco-Lao schools for the Lao adults that later expanded to include a system of elementary education for children. The pagoda schools were forced to merge with the newly created system. A teachers college was organized to retrain Laotian monks to teach in the Lao secular system in 1909.[9] In 1917, the French proclaimed the Lao schools as a part of a common Indochina education system that also included Cambodia and Vietnam. This means that Lao students could pursue further studies in Hanoi, Saigon, or Phnom-Penh or vice versa.[10]

In terms of teaching and learning, because there was such a shortage of the French-speaking Laotians, teachers were initially French with imported French-speaking Vietnamese instructors from Vietnam serving as substitutes. French was the instructional and official language of Laos until the 1960's. In 1939, an official order from the French colonial administration in Laos required that every community in Laos build a "village school" and a "teacher house." The French government supplied the teachers and the materials.[11] However, there was no report on the progress of how this order was implemented.

It was reported that about 1,000 students enrolled in 1920 and 7,000 in 1930. Perhaps the Great Depression of the 1930's had little effect on the underdeveloped countries such as Laos as denoted by the marginal decline in school enrollment from 7,000 to 6,700. Despite this report, two additional conflicting sources were also reported. The first one indicated that student enrollment at the elementary school level in Laos, instead of declining as previously reported, was doubled since the 1930s. As a result, student enrollment increased from 6,700 to 14,700 from 1939 to 1946.[12] In the meantime, a second source revealed that there were roughly 24,047 students, 704 teachers, and 569 elementary schools in 1946.[13] However, there was no explanation as to why there is a discrepancy between the numbers of students between these two sources.

The French colonization brought the entry of the European model to Laos at the secondary education level. In 1925, Auguste Pavie founded the Pavie College, the first high school in Laos, for the elite families. About twenty Lao families were considered in this indigenous group. They were trained academically in the French style and language to be civil servants. Pavie College (a high school) was also supplemented by provincial secondary schools located in Pakse, Luang Prabang, and Savannakhet two decades later. Provo reported that, in 1946, about

200 students enrolled at the secondary level.[14] Noss claimed that the first and only high school in Vientiane was founded in 1921 and did not become a full lycee until 1949.[15] A lycee is a French public secondary school. Thee made an interesting observation that only ten Laotians graduated from high schools in France and Hanoi during the French rule.[16]

French-Mong Relationship

In addition to education, other social events shaped the relationship between the Mong and French. There were two main events that earned the Mong a recognition and a close relationship with the French. In 1885, Vietnamese Emperor Ham Nghi and his advisor, Ton That Thuyet, rebelled against the French. Both men sought refuge in the highlands of Laos. The Mong were used as scouts to successfully capture Ham Nghi and Ton That Thuyet.

The second main event was marked by the Treaty of Tien Tshin between France and China in 1884. The treaty forced China to recognize French sovereignty over Vietnam. However, Chinese garrisons continued to occupy various sectors of the frontier, and the Chinese became warlords and bandits known as "the Black Flags." Aided by the Mong for a period of over thirty years from 1884-1914, the French were able to push the Black Flags back to China.[17]

Nevertheless, the relationship between the French and the Mong deteriorated. In 1916, the French applied several taxes in Laos. An annual per capita tax along with a semi-annual tax was implemented in Laos. These taxes were collected either in monetary form or in the form of goods. Further, every Mong household was to devote two-weeks free labor for road construction from Laos to Vietnam. The free labor which soon increased from two weeks to months to a year disrupted the Mong's farming season. Many Mong were unable to cultivate the land in time for farming. As a result, at the end of the year, many Mong families faced starvation. When the year ended during the tax collection period, they were unable to pay their taxes to the French. Many Mong families had to pawn their children as slaves to pay the taxes. This tax burden led to anti-French dissatisfaction among the Mong throughout Laos. The great rebellion known as the "*Rog Phim Bab*" (Mad War) which was led by Pa Chay against the French lasted for six years from 1917 to 1922.[18]

World War II

World War II itself did not have much impact on the Mong. During World War II, Laos was occupied by the Japanese from 1941-1945. In 1945, the Japanese occupation force in Asia took complete control over the French colonial administration in Laos and forced King Sisavangvong to proclaim independence from France. Touby Lyfoung led the Mong to join the French in guerrilla warfare against the Japanese. Because this war period was quite short, the Japanese had very little influence on the education of the Mong. Many Mong vividly remembered World War II as "*Rog Yiv Poos*" (the Japanese War).

The aftermath of World War II had a tremendous effect on the future of the Mong. Perhaps it had changed the Mong society forever. After World War II, new nations were born in Africa and Asia from the old colonial empires.[19] Laos gained independence from France in 1949 and established a constitutional monarchy.

The Cold War

The end of World War II signaled the beginning of psychological warfare between the United States and the Soviet Union referred to as "the Cold War." Perhaps, the emergence of the Cold War was the turning point for change in the Mong society. It was one of the global trends that affected the Mong the most. The United States and the Soviet Union had two competing and different political systems. The United States believed in democracy. The Soviet Union asserted Communism in Eastern Europe and Asia as a buffer to provide for its security. While Western Europe's economy was unstable, many subversive activities were strongly supported by the Communists in France. The nations of the world were divided into a bipolar world: those associated with the United States joined as the North Atlantic Treaty Organization (NATO) allies and those with the Soviet Union as the Warsaw Pact.

Between 1946-1948, operating within the context of the Truman doctrine, Secretary of State George Marshall devised massive military and economic aid to foreign governments in Western Europe. This aid was known as the "Marshall Plan" with a goal to build and to strengthen the military and economy of Western Europe.[20] In addition, to prevent the Communist expansion into the world, George Kennan, a long time student of Russia, formulated the "Containment Policy." This policy was to keep the Soviet Union contained in Eastern Europe without spreading to various regions of Europe.[21]

The Cold War became intensified between the United States and the Soviet Union. President Truman stated:

> Given a choice between freedom and totalitarianism, it must be the policy of the United States to support free peoples who are resisting attempted subjugation by armed minorities.[22]

The Marshall plan worked well in Europe but similar strategies did not work in Asia where China became Communist. The Cold War and its global effects were conceivably the cause for the external political instability in Vietnam and for the elongated internal tripartite conflict within Laos (discussed later in this chapter).

Vietnam War

Vietnam was part of the French colonization in Southeast Asia. After World War II, Vietnam gained full independence from France. However, two political parties existed within Vietnam. The south, led by *Ngo Dinh Diem*, supported democracy while the north was led by *Ho Chi Minh*, a nationalist and a proponent of Communism.[23] President Eisenhower provided the initial military and economic aid to the South Vietnamese government which commenced the United States' involvement in the Vietnam conflict. Aid was expanded under President John F. Kennedy. Then, the United States became heavily involved in this aid under President Lyndon B. Johnson and President Richard M. Nixon.

In the 1950's, "the Domino Theory" emerged. It was premised on a constant fear of the rapid expansion of Communism into the world. Influenced by Secretary of State John Foster Dulles, President Dwight Eisenhower declared that:

> You have a row of dominoes set up, you knock over the first one and what will happen to the last one is certainly that it will go over very quickly.[24]

During the Eisenhower Administration, only military officers and advisers were sent to Vietnam to build a conventional fighting force for the South Vietnamese government. This support was doubled under the Kennedy Administration when the United States deployed 16,000 troops in South Vietnam in 1963. The Johnson Administration deepened its involvement by increasing the American troops to 23,000 and contemplated direct strikes against North Vietnam.[25]

In 1964, the North Vietnamese Communists attacked US destroyers in the Gulf of Tonkin. This attack is disputed as to whether it was real or staged to give the US a reason to escalate the war. President Johnson ordered the bombing of North Vietnam. This marked the debut for the US engagement in the Vietnam conflict that lasted for ten years from 1964 to 1974.

Mong Involvement With the Vietnam War

The Vietnam conflict between the 1960s and the 1970s had a direct consequence on the lives of the Mong and on the political instability of Laos. When the United States became involved in the Vietnam Conflict, there was a lot of resistance against the Communists from the South Vietnamese forces. The US troops were also stationed along the seventeenth parallel. This made it very difficult for the Vietnamese Communists to transport their troops, food, and ammunition to support their ground fighting squads in South Vietnam.

In addition, in 1962, twelve countries including the United States and North Vietnam signed the Geneva Accord of 1962 in Switzerland to guarantee the neutrality of Laos. Since the Vietnamese Communists could not transport their troops, ammunition and food directly to South Vietnam along the seventeen parallel, they cut a new route in northern Laos -- Route 13 known as the "*Ho-Chi-Minh Trail*" where the Mong lived to support their fighting troops in South Vietnam.

By continuing to send their troops through the "*Ho-Chi-Minh Trail*" to South Vietnam, the Vietnamese Communists breached the Geneva Accord of 1962. The US Central Intelligence Agency (CIA) approached the Mong General Vang Pao and the Mong to fight this war. In a videotaped interview with Su Thao in 1995, General Harry C. Aderholt acknowledged that he and Bill Lair representing the United States made several trips to Padong, Xieng Khouang, Laos in January, October, and November of 1960 to convince Captain Vang Pao and the Mong to assist the US government to fight the Vietnamese Communists. They made a verbal agreement that if things did not work out, the United States would provide a safe place for the Mong and their families.[26] As a result, General Vang Pao formed a special force known as "The US Secret Army in Laos."

General Vang Pao specified the two missions as follows: First was to strategically penetrate the Communist force by reducing their troops, ammunition, and food along the Ho-Chi-Minh Trail. Second was to provide general and special rescue missions to downed American pilots.[27] The Mong sometimes sacrificed as many as ten or more lives just to save one downed American pilot. Long Tieng, the Second Military Division of the Royal Lao Army, was the headquarter of this operation:

> It [Long Tieng] was the most forward advanced command post in Laos of the United States Air Force, which directed secret bombing missions first into North Vietnam and then all over Laos itself from buildings beside a milelong, all-weather macadam runway, the only field in northeast Laos capable of handling jet aircraft in trouble.[28]

The US Secret Army force consisted of 25,000 men of the royal army of Laos. The majority of the force were Mong. They were organized, trained, paid, and entirely supported by the United States through the command of Brigadier General John A. Heintges and his 400 "technicians.[29] Many CIA agents and military advisors known as "the Green Berets" whose names perhaps remained anonymous were stationed in Long Tieng, Laos. Out of these, two Americans whom the Mong will remember distinctly for a long time were Colonel Jerry Daniels from Montana known as "Jerry" and particularly Edgar Pop Buell from Indiana known as "*Thanh Pad*" or "Mister Pop." They were distinguished by their profound and personal dedication to the Mong even long after the fall of the Laotian government to the Communists. As the only remaining military advisor to the Mong, Colonel Daniels was so memorable to the Mong because he immersed himself into the Mong people for about two decades and adopted their culture as his. As visible as he was among the Mong and Southeast Asians, he was not afraid to be with the Mong but spoke for the Mong and fought along side the Mong. Along the same line, Buell was recognized for his humanistic commitment to the Mong. Buell made a bipartisan pledge to General Vang Pao that:

> I [Buell] and you [Vang Pao] will just have our own counter-insurgency program right here [Pha Khao]. You take care of the military, and I'll take care of the civilians. And if I'm going to take care of 'em, I'd better be the one who goes out and finds 'em.[30]

In the 1960's, Buell, a farmer near Metz, Indiana, joined a private peace corps conducted under contract to the Government's Point Four AID program in Laos.[31] Buell organized an emergency relief program to airlift and to drop the necessary life-saving supplies to displaced Mong through Air America. Schanche described that Air America:

> was the private airline of the Central Intelligence Agency, used throughout Southeast Asia to support intelligence operatives in the fields.[32]

The cost of the relief program for all Laos ran about $4.5 million a year. The additional costs per year were $8.8 million for air transportation, $1.5 million for public health, and $1.25 million for education.[33]

Impact of the US Secret Army in Laos on Mong Education

The impact of this war (the US Secret Army in Laos) was devastating to the Mong. From 1960 to 1965, the numbers of casualties were enormous. It was estimated that 40,000 people or ten percent of the population of northeast Laos had either been killed or died due to war injuries.[34] Many innocent children as young as fourteen were drafted to the military to bear arms.

Education of the Mong children was disrupted because of the constant fighting and movement of the Mong. Schanche asserted that the development of educational programs for thousands of displaced Mong refugees during the Vietnam War was made possible through Buell's efforts. The first school was built in Ban Na in 1961 with twenty-seven pupils. By the end of 1961, a total of twenty-eight elementary schools were constructed. By 1969, the school system expanded to nine Groupes Scolaires (junior high schools), two high schools, and a teacher training school. About 300 Mong students enrolled in French high schools in Vientiane. Another seventy enrolled in the local Lao-American school and two dozens in universities across the world.[35]

Commemoration of the Mong Veterans

On July 22, 1995, several key individuals in the Mong-American communities and US officials were involved in the planning for the Commemoration of the Mong veterans taken place in Denver, Colorado. These individuals included Yang Chee, Colonel Hang Sao, Colonel William "Bill" F. Bilodeaux, Christine Cook, and the American Tribute Committee with the cooperation of Colonel Frank Bales, General Harry C. Aderholt, General Jim Hall, General Steve Ritchie, General Art Cornelius, and the Mong veterans nationwide. They put together a special tribute to commemorate the 40,000 Mong soldiers who died in the U.S. Secret Army in Laos and 15,000 Mong soldiers who were wounded in the line of duty between 1961-1975 during the Vietnam conflict. This was the first event in the history of the United States that recognized and honored the Mong veterans who dedicated their service in support of the American Armed Forces of the United States of America during the Vietnam War. Colonel Hang Sao, Dr. Dao Yang, Colonel Nhia Lue Vang, Colonel Xay Dang Xiong, and Colonel Tou Long Yang along with many Mong veterans throughout the nation accepted the thirty-eight symbolic medals of awards on behalf of the Mong soldiers who died in the war and the Mong veterans. In this event, General Jim Hall read a proclamation from the Congress of the United States, House of Representatives, Washington, DC, dated 20 July 1995 with the citation as follows:

> On behalf of a grateful people of the United States of America and the citizens of Colorado, we award today to the Lao-Mong (the Defenders of Freedom Citation) in honor of dedicated service and support of the American Armed Forces of the United States of America during the Vietnam War. This citation is in recognition of outstanding performance of duty in action against enemy forces of Military Region II, in his (Lao-Mong) native country of Laos. He (Lao-Mong) successfully executed primary missions for air support and combat logistic support for United States Military forces to include the rescuing of American air personnel during the battles in the theater of operations. It further commemorates

the Lao-Hmong of Military Region II, in Laos, during the war in the
Vietnam conflict.

The medal is inscribed as follows:

In honor of those men and women who gave themselves in an effort to
ensure democracy and peace throughout the world, this medal is
instructed by acts of Congress 1984. I commend you for your bravery
and loyalty to the United States of America.

Signed by Dan Schaffer
Member of Congress
Sixth District of Colorado[36]

Christianity and Mong Literacy Development

Many Mong became Christians through the mission of the Christian
and Missionary Alliance (CMA) headquartered in New York (now in
Colorado Springs, Colorado). Rev. Xuxu Thao, the first Mong
president of the Lao Evangelical Church during 1964-1967, revered the
memory of the history of the Mong Church in Laos. Rev. Audetat
along with Gabriel Contesse and the Wiley's, the earlier missionaries
from the Swiss Brethren Assemblies, brought the Gospel of Christ to
the village of Song Khone, Savannakhet, southern Laos in 1902,
mastered the Lao language, and completed the first translation of the
Lao version of the Bible. Since the Lao were long influenced by Indian
Buddhism (the same concept of Hindu Buddhism presented previously
in this chapter), it was difficult to convert them to Christianity. The
Kounthapanyas was one of the first few Laotian families to convert to
Christianity. Twenty-five years later, in 1928, a Canadian missionary
couple, the Roffes, went to Luang Prabang, the Royal capital city of
Laos, where the king of Laos resided. The couple mastered the Lao
language and refined the translation of the earlier Lao biblical version in
the 1950's.

The massive Mong and Khamu conversion took place in 1950
when the Andrianoffes went to Xieng Khouang province of Laos. After
converting the first Khamu, Nai Kheng, the Andrianoffes rented a house
for him and for their Laotian translator, Nai U-Tee. The house once
belonged to a French couple, the Besons, who lived and died there.
The Besons' home (known as the haunted house) was located at Phou
Kham in Xieng Khouang, Laos, where Bua Ya Thao (the shaman of
Touby Lyfoung), You Xang Thao, and Chong Her Thao's families
lived. The fact that the Beson's ghosts did not seem to bother Nai
Kheng and Nai U-Tee shocked shaman Bua Ya Thao. Bua Ya Thao
decided that if ghosts did not bother Christians, he would become a
Christian and therefore be protected from ghosts. Bua Ya Thao was the
first Mong convert to Christianity in Laos followed by You Xang Thao

and Chong Her Thao's. This incident of the Besons' haunted house perhaps set the stage for the massive conversion of the Mong in the following three years. In the same year, the Andrianoffes and Nai Kheng traveled to Phou Kabo, Kiao Kouang villages followed by twenty other Mong, and to fifteen Khamu villages to convert 5,000 Mong and 2,000 Khamu to Christianity. The numbers of converts totaled approximately 7,000 from 1950 through 1953.

Thao indicated that the Mong had been longing for the future King of the Mong - a Messiah - who possessed supernatural and magical power to save the Mong from the power of the devils and from natural calamity, and to uplift the socio-economic conditions of the Mong. Christianity appeared to be the answer.[37] Thao further asserted that there were many factors that might have set the stage for the massive conversion of the Mong and Khamu tribes to Christianity. These factors included:

1. Between 1940-1945, some Mong soothsayers, such as Mrs. Xay Sue Thao and Mrs. Youa Yao Thao, told the Mong to stop worshipping the devils;
2. Between 1940-1945, some Mong soothsayers commanded the Mong to stop opium and alcohol use and predicted religious change;
3. Between 1940-1945, a Mong legend emerged. It characterized a Mong by the name of "*Chu Xang*" *(Tswv Xyaas)*. Through his magical knowledge, he placed a bamboo basket on his head and a pair of sickles in his mouth, then transformed himself into a tiger to hunt wild animals for food. One day, he erroneously killed a Khamu woman. Therefore, the Mong were frightened to take the basket off his head and the pair of sickles out of his mouth. After that *Chu Xang (Tswv Xyaas)* became a real tiger and traveled to the frontier of China to challenge the Black Tiger for the White Dirt territory. The White Dirt territory was avoided by Mong because it was a deep jungle area, inhabited only by animals. Due to his smaller physical size, Chu Xang was defeated by the Black Tiger. He returned to Laos to recruit the souls of many talented, intellectual, and well-known Mong in Xieng Khouang to assist him during his struggle against the Black Tiger. As a result, many Mong died due to *Chu Xang's* spiritual recruitment. If a Mong were Christian, he was saved from being spiritually recruited by *Chu Xang* and being forced to go to the White Dirt territory by *Chu Xang*;
4. The Mong were exposed to the power of black magic of the Khamu and the Laotians. This scenario worried many Mong. Whenever a Mong went down to the valleys, he normally died after returning home. Perhaps the instantaneous change in climate may have

affected their physical being, but the Mong believed their deaths were the result of black magic;

5. Several cholera epidemics hit the Mong. Traditionally, it is customary for the Mong males to bury the dead. Thao recounted that in one year the numbers of dead were so many that Mong women had to perform burials;

6. The Khamu were also hit hard by another natural calamity, fire. Thao estimated that as many as twenty Khamu villages caught fire simultaneously (within three months) one village after another. According to the Khamu, they believed that becoming Christians would save them from this type of natural phenomenon.

Another factor that might have set the stage for the massive conversion of the Mong and Khamu to Christianity was the economic, political, and educational changes in 1951. Barney, a missionary to Xieng Khouang, Laos, witnessed Mong participation in local trade, engagement in wage labor, "lease terraced fields for irrigated rice farming," an enculturation toward inquiry and adoption of new ideas, augmentation in the political realm of Laotian national government, and participation in greater opportunities in education. Some Mong even went to *Lycee* in Vientiane. Barney knew at least one who attended college in Saigon.[38] This economic, political, and educational change along with the emergence of Christianity in Laos made some of the Mong accept that Jesus Christ as the King of the Mong - the Messiah mentioned previously. They believed Jesus had power over the spirits of nature based on their life experiences with the Besons' ghosts, the Chu Xang's experience, natural calamity, and many other factors described above.

One of the immediate issues faced by the Christian and Missionary Alliance (CMA) was the illiteracy of the Mong and the Khamu tribes. They could neither read nor write Lao. Both tribes had no writing systems of their own. Rev. Xeng Pao Thao, the second Mong president of the Lao Evangelical Church in 1968-1970, discussed the origin of the development of Mong literacy. In 1951, about ninety percent of the Christians in Laos were Mong. According to Rev. Xeng Pao Thao, Mong Leng (Blue Mong) accounted for about ninety percent of the Mong Christians. Because of their massive conversion to Christianity, CMA conducted several conferences in 1951, 1952 and 1953. The conference resolution assigned two missionaries the tasks of developing writing systems for the Mong and the Khamu tribes. In this manner, Christian literacy and Bible translation could be developed in Mong and Khamu. In turn, recent converts could comprehend the Christian doctrines which were the roots and the foundation of the Christian faith.

As a result of the resolution, Barney went to Xieng Khouang to study Mong Leng (Blue Mong) and Smalley to Luang Prabang to study Khamu.[39] Barney acknowledged that, in June 1951, he "set the task of reducing the Mong language to writing."[40] Smalley also confirmed this mission.[41] Barney mastered the Mong language and Romanized it into the Romanized Popular Alphabet (RPA) System. Many Mong called him *"Thanh Mong"* or "Mister Mong." Smalley, trained as a linguist, after completing his work in Khamu, assisted Barney to refine the RPA system for the Mong as well.[42] In 1953, the Communists took over Xieng Khouang province. All missionaries had to be evacuated for a short period of time so the Mong research project was interrupted. When the RPA system was completed, it was submitted to the Lao government in 1954 for approval but it was repudiated for political reasons.

The Christian and Missionary Alliance established a Bible School and a church in the province of Xieng Khouang. Their activities focused mainly on the administration of the Bible School. By early 1953, there were about 3,000 Christians living in fifty-six villages. At the end of the Communist hostilities, the numbers of Christians increased to 5,000 or 6,000 living in ninety-six villages. The Mong accounted for about seventy percent of the Christian believers in Laos.[43]

In 1962, Miss Doris Whitelock of the Overseas Missionary Fellowship (OMF) in Thailand visited the Mong Christians in Laos and informed them of the Thai orthography for Mong. This Thai-based system was developed by Doris Whitelock in Thailand. She used the Thai orthography to write Mong. Upon knowing the system, the Lao Evangelical Church requested Miss Whitelock to assist the Mong language Christian Literacy Committee to prepare a Lao orthography for Mong in 1966 and completed the system in 1968. This committee consisted of Rev. Yong Xeng Yang, Rev. Nha Yee Kong, Rev. Cheng Xiong and Rev. Nhia Neng Her. The first Mong Bible translation using the Lao orthography was completed in August 1975 when the majority of Mong became refugees in *Nam Phong* refugee camp, Udorn, Thailand. The numbers of Mong Christians increased to 15,000. In March 1977, Rev. Xeng Pao Thao, acting President of the Lao Evangelical Church, requested Miss Doris Whitelock and Rev. Wayne Persons (also known as "Paaj Tsaab Vaaj") to switch the Lao orthography for Mong to the Romanized Popular Alphabet (RPA) system due to the fact that the Mong no longer lived in Laos.[44]

In 1987, Rev. Xuxu Thao reminisced some of the major accomplishments, which accounted for the development of Christianity in Laos, particularly among the Mong from 1950 to 1975 as follows:

1. A Lao Bible Training School was established in Vientiane in 1961 to train over 100 Mong and other tribal pastors. As a result, most of the Mong pastors, Christian laymen, and Mong leaders who are in the United States today are the products of this training;

2. A church in the "Saphangmo" area was built in Vientiane, Laos to accommodate the commuting Mong Christians and the US officials who were detailed in Vientiane. The US officials made up a fairly large American congregation;
3. Dormitories, built for Mong students and Mong widows, were partially funded by World Vision of Laos;
4. A private Christian school, "Saphangmo Christian School," was also built by the funds of World Council of Churches to admit over 300 students in the area;
5. The Lao Evangelical Church completed the translation of two Mong Bible versions (one in Blue Mong and one in White Hmong) in Lao orthography;
6. The Lao Evangelical Church purchased a cemetery in the area of Nong Tha, Vientiane, Laos;
7. Furthermore, the Lao Evangelical Church worked closely with the Church of Christ in Thailand and other countries between 1965-1973 to develop future leaders for the Lao Evangelical Church. Seven Mong and two Laotians were selected to continue their education abroad. They were Vang Sue, Moua Chou, Moua Lee, Bee Thao, Vang Lue, Koua Thao, Douangnary Kounthapanya, Malay Kounthapanya, and Paoze Thao (the author).[45]

Internal Tripartite Conflict

When Laos gained its independence from France, its politicians were caught in between the Allies and Communism in the midst of the military, political, and psychological battleground of the continuing "Cold War" developed by the United States and the Soviet Union. In order to survive in the world politics and to protect Laos from being colonized by the Western countries again, Laos sided with neither the Allies nor the Communists. The Cold War forced Laos to devise strategic and political mechanisms for the survival of the country. Perhaps neutrality was the alternative, so Laos established a neutral political system consisting of three political parties: the Neutralist party, the Right Wing party, and the Neo Lao Hatsat or the Pathet Lao (the proponent of Socialism and Communism). Each party wanted to establish political stability in Laos, but only in the party's own way. Therefore, the Laotians were divided into three major groups.

Laos' political fate depended upon two royal half-brother princes: Chao Souvannaphouma (the neutral political party leader) and Chao Souphanouvong (the Neo Lao Hatsat- the proponent of the Communist left wing party leader). Despite the establishment of neutrality for the country, Laos was caught in between the policy of Communist expansion of the Soviet Union and the containment policy of the United States. The conflict between the three factions resulted in a long tripartite civil war that lasted for the following four decades until 1975. This endless guerrilla warfare continued to trouble Laos as the three factions fought against one another, one coup d'etat after another, which continued to impact all aspects of life in Laos. The following illustrates the internal tripartite war within Laos.

In 1957, the three political parties (the Right Wing party– proponents of democracy, the Neutral party – proponents of neutrality and the Left Wing party – proponents of Socialism and Communism) in the Lao government formed a coalition government of national union. This coalition government lasted only for a few months. The Right Wing political party, supported by the US CIA, seized power. The Pathet Lao leaders were incarcerated by General Phoumi Nosavan of the Right Wing political party and established a Right Wing government. In August 1960, the government formed by Right Wing political party in Vientiane, Laos. Then, it was overthrown by the Neutral Political party. This neutralist coup d'etat which was led by General Kong Le[46] installed Prince Souvannaphouma to head the neutral government as Prime Minister. Prince Souvannaphouma served as Prime Minister until 1975.[47] In December 1960, four months later, General Phoumi Nosavan attacked the capital city, Vientiane and set the stage for a full scale civil war. By 1961, two-thirds of Laos was under the control of the Pathet Lao and the neutralist forces.[48]

The 1954 Geneva Agreements ended the French rule in Laos, but the United States replaced the French instead. The following supported this claim. According to Toye, Secretary of State John Foster Dulles proclaimed that Laos was under the protection of the South East Asia Treaty Organization (SEATO). The US opened the United States Operation Mission (USOM) office in Laos in 1955.[49] In 1960, President Eisenhower approved the secret use of the United States and Thai Air forces in the civil war. When John F. Kennedy became president, he viewed Laos as the gate to Asia and a testing ground for peace in our world.[50] On July 23, 1962, twelve countries including the United States, the Soviet Union and North Vietnam signed the Geneva Accords in Switzerland to guarantee Laos as a neutral and independent country to be ruled under the tripartite government formed by the Right Wing, the Neutralists and the Pathet Lao.[52]

The Laotian people, known as peace-loving people, causing nobody any harm, wanted to establish peace among themselves. However, the wars changed their attitudes over time. Wolfkill, an American news photographer with NBC, wanted to witness the peace agreement scheduled to be held in the province of Vang Vieng, Laos and described the Laotians as:

> the most gentle, most peace-loving people on earth. Buddhists, they hesitated to kill even animals, much less each other.

Captured by the Pathet Lao forces in 1961 and held in brutal captivity for fifteen months, Wolfkill perceived that the war forced the Laotian people to change their attitudes over time.[51] In addition, Dengler, an example of the American servicemen, who experienced the brutality of being a prisoner of war. In February 1966, he was shot down half way across Laos, was captured by the Pathet Lao, was sent to a prison camp, and then successfully escaped from Laos.[55] Therefore, wars can change charming, peace-loving individuals' attitudes over time.

The Communist North Vietnamese breached the Geneva Accord of 1962 by building up troops in Pathet Lao territory along the Ho-Chi-Minh Trail to South Vietnam. In response, Prime Minister Souvannaphouma requested American economic and military aid. The result was large scale air operations over Northern Laos especially in Xieng Khouang where the Mong lived. It was reported that over 25,000 missions were flown against *Les Plaines des Jarres* (the Plains of Jars) from May 1964 through September 1969. It was estimated that over 75,000 tons of bombs were dropped and over 50,000 airmen at distant bases were involved.[53] Even though thousands of people were killed and wounded and the Plains of Jars (Plaines des Jarres) may have disappeared forever, the massive bombardment was kept secret from the world. If it had been publicized, the United States could have been known to breach the Geneva Accords of 1962. The battles in Laos became so severe that, in February 1971, three specific battalions of the South Vietnamese army in South Vietnam under the command of Lieutenant General Lam were ordered to clear the Ho-Chi-Minh Trail.[56] The war in Laos was described by many witnesses as the "Ugly Duckling or the Seesaw War."[57]

The American airmen who fought this secret war were known as "the Ravens." Their missions were "to fly low and slow, spot the enemy, and direct the winged artillery of American air strikes from adjacent South Vietnam, Thailand and U.S. aircraft carriers." Robbins asserted that the stories of the Ravens during the Vietnam conflict were locked away in classified archives. They would not be revealed until after the year 2000.[54]

Laos may have been used as a testing ground for chemical warfare first by the United States between the 1960s to the 1970s and later by the former Soviet Union after 1975. This testing ground occurred during their competition for the leading role in the arms race during the Cold War. Bruchett in his *Second Indochina War* reported that the tonnage of bombs that were dropped on Lao villages exceeded that dropped in any year on North Vietnam. It was more than on Nazi-occupied Europe in World War II.[58] After 1975, the former Soviet Union used aerial attacks with gas rockets of different types - yellow, green or red - on the territory where the Mong lived, that caused headaches, vomiting, diarrhea, and death after being exposed to those gases.[59] Many Mong referred to this phenomenon as the "Yellow Rain." External support from Communist China and North Vietnam to the Pathet Lao made it impossible for the Laotians to resolve their internal tripartite conflict. Because the United States viewed Laos as the gateway to Asia under the Southeast Asian Treaty Organization (SEATO), the Chinese regarded the U.S. commitment to Laos as a threat to its national security. The Chinese shifted a moderate policy aiming at a neutralized Laos to a militant one by supporting the Pathet Lao's military activities. Lee reported that in 1966, the Chinese concentrated more than 300,000 troops and several air force units in the province of Yunnan and Kwangshi just north of Vietnam and Laos.[60] Therefore, the idea of establishing a political ideology of neutrality in the world was never realized for Laos.

Neo-Colonialism

During the Neo-Colonialism period (1948-1961), Laos adopted the structure of government from France. Under the constitution, the King was the Head of State with his Judicial Council. The National Assembly formed the legislative authority. His royal Chief Executive was the Prime Minister who served as the president of the Council of Ministers. The Council of Ministers consisted of nine ministers and four Secretaries of State. The country was divided into sixteen provinces under the territorial organization. The principal administrative division was the *Khoueng* (province) headed by the provincial governor, who exercised his authority under the direction of the Minister of Interior. Then, the *Khoueng* was divided into *Muong* (cities), *Kong* (head of ethnic minority groups), *Tasseng* (districts), and *Ban* (villages).

Summary

Chapter 3 has examined the trends that shaped Mong society and has identified their significant impact on the Mong during their settlement in Laos. These trends included French colonialism, World War II, Vietnam War, Christianity and Mong literacy development, and the internal tripartite conflict, and their implication on education.

Chapter 4 will examine the rationale why the Mong fled from Laos to seek asylum in Thailand and then to the United States for resettlement. Their cultural problems will be identified relative to their resettlement in the United States.

Notes

[1] Jean Mottin, *History of the Hmong* (Bangkok: Odeon Store, Ltd., 1978), 50.
[2] Human Relations Area Files, *Laos: its People, its Society, its Culture* (New Haven: Hraf Press, 1960), 1.
[3] Maha Sila Viravong, *History of Laos* (New York: Paragon Book Reprint Corp., 1964), 6:83 and 7:109.
[4] T.D. Roberts, et al., *Area Handbook for Laos* (Washington, D.C.: U.S. Government Printing Office, 1967), 128-129.
[5] Ibid., 129.
[6] D.J.M. Tate, *The Making of Modern South-East Asia*, Vol. I (Kualalumpur, Singapore: Oxford University Press, 1971), 487-495.
[7] Human Area Relations Files, 15-18.
[8] T.D. Roberts, et al., 26-27.
[9] Ibid., 107-108.
[10] Ibid., 107-108.
[11] Human Relations Area Files, *Laos: its People, its Society, its Culture* (New Haven: Hraf Press, 1967), 80.
[12] Human Relations Area Files, 78-81.
[13] G. Provo, *Laos: Programmes et Manuel Scolaires*, UNESCO, No. de series: 1255/BMS.RD/EDM, (Paris: UNESCO, 1969), 8.
[14] Ibid., 8.
[15] Richard Noss, *Higher Education and Development in South-east Asia*, Vol. III Part 2: Language Policy and Higher Education (Paris: United Nations Educational, Scientific and Cultural Organizations, and the International Association of Universities, 1967), VIII: 123.
[16] Marek Thee, *Notes of a Witness : Laos and the Second Indochinese War* (New York: Vintage Books Edition, 1973), 10.
[17] Keith Quincy, *Hmong: History of a People* (Cheney, Washington: Eastern Washington University Press, 1988), 112-118.
[18] Ibid., 119-129.
[19] Philip H. Coombs, *The World Crisis in Education: The View from the Eighties* (New York: Oxford University Press, 1985), 3.
[20] Ibid., 3 and 68-70.
[21] William A. Chafe, *The Unfinished Journey* (New York: Oxford Press, 1968), 3:68.
[22] Ibid., 67.
[23] U.S. Department of Justice, Immigration and Naturalization Service, *United States History: 1600-1987* (Washington, D.C.: U.S. Government Printing Office, 1988), 131-134.
[24] Chafe, 258.
[25] Ibid., 278.
[26] Interview with General Harry C. Aderholt by Su Thao, videotaping, at the Commemoration for the Mong Veteran Memorial Award in Denver, Colorado, 22 July 1995 in S.T. Universal Studio, *Ncu Txug Txaj Ntsig Moob* [Commemoration of the Mong Veterans] (Fresno, California: S.T. Universal Studio, 1995 and 1996), Part I and Part II.

[27] Testimony of General Vang Pao at the Mong New Year Celebration, DesMoines, Iowa, 29 November 1980; and Conversation with General Vang Pao during the Trip to Hamilton, Indiana to attend Edgar Pop Buell's Funeral, 5-6 January, 1981.
[28] Don A. Schanche, *Mister Pop* (New York: David McKay Company, Inc., 1970), 263.
[29] Ibid., 2:21-22.
[30] Ibid., 103.
[31] Ibid., 20.
[32] Ibid., 81.
[33] Ibid., 246.
[34] Ibid., 245.
[35] Ibid., Schanche, p. 93.
[36] Su Thao, *Ncu Txug Txajntsig Moob II* [Commemoration of the Mong Veterans], videotaping, at the Commemoration for the Mong Veteran Memorial Award in Denver, Colorado, 22 July 1995 (Fresno California: S.T. Universal Video, 1996), Part II.
[37] Interview with Rev. Xuxu Thao, tape recording, "The History of the Lao Evangelical Church," Ottawa, Illinois, 1 January, 1987.
[38] George L. Barney, "Christianity: Innovation in Meo Culture," (MA Thesis, University of Minnesota, 1957), 3:50-56.
[39] Interview with Rev. Xeng Pao Thao, tape recording, "History of the Development of Mong Literacy," Madison Heights, Michigan, 18 February 1984.
[40] Barney, 4:68.
[41] William A. Smalley. "History of the Development of the Hmong Literacy." Presentation to the Hmong Language Council. University of Minnesota, 12 August, 1982.
[42] William A. Smalley, ed. "The Problems of Consonants and Tone: Hmong (Meo, Miao)," *Phonemes and Orthography: Language Planning in Ten Minority Languages of Thailand* (Pacific Linguistics Series C. No. 43) (Canberra: Australian National University), 4: 85-123.
[43] Barney, 68-69.
[44] Xeng Pao Thao, Interview.
[45] Xuxu Thao, interview.
[46] Thee, 12.
[47] Hugh Toye, *Laos: Buffer State or Battleground* (London: Oxford University Press, 1968), 138-170.
[48] Thee, 12-13.
[49] Ibid., 12.
[50] Ibid., 12-14.
[52] Carl Berger, *The United States Air Force in Southeast Asia* (Washington, D.C.: Office of Air Force History, 1977), preface and 121-135.
[51] Grant Wolfkill, *Reported to Be Alive* (New York: Simon & Schuster, 1965), 12.
[55] Dieter Dengler, *Escape From Laos* (San Rafael, CA: Presidio Press, 1979), 7-13, 15-25, 91-112, and 113-134.

[53] Frederic Branfman, *Voices from the Plain of Jars: Life under an Air War* (New York: Harper Colophon Books, 1972), 4.

[56] Keith William Nolan, *Into Laos: Dewey Canyon II/Lam Son 719* (Novato, CA: Presidio Press, 1986), 103.

[57] Robert Shaplen, *Time out of Hand: Revolution and Reaction in Southeast Asia* (New York: Harper & Row, Publishers, 1962), 343.

[54] Christopher Robbins, *The Ravens: The Men Who Flew in America's Secret War in Laos* (New York: Crown Publisher, Inc., 1978), 2.

[58] Wilfred G. Bruchett, *The Second Indochina War: Cambodia and Laos* (New York: International Publishers, 1970), 168.

[59] Jean Larteguy, *La Fabuleuse Aventure du Peuple de l'Opium* (Eure, France: Presses de la Cite, 1979), 253.

[60] Chae-Jin Lee, *Communist China's Policy Toward Laos: A Case Study, 1954-67* (Lawrence, Kansas: Center for East Asian Studies, the University of Kansas, 1970), 1-12.

Chapter 4

Mong Resettlement in the United States

This chapter will examine the rationale why the Mong people migrated from Laos to the United States, how they seek asylum in Thailand and how they came to the United States for resettlement. The chapter will probe the refugee registration process, the Refugee Act of 1980, and resettlement process by the Voluntary Agencies (VOLAGs). This chapter will also provide a general description of the Southeast Asian ethnic groups coming to the United States and problems of cultural and educational adjustment of the Mong in the United States.

Prior to 1975, very few Mong were in the United States. They were the family members of General Vang Pao and the Mong students who received scholarships and came to the United States to continue their education. The fall of the Laotian government to the Communists in May 1975 resulted in a massive Mong exodus to Thailand for first asylum, then to the United States and other countries in the Western hemisphere for relocation. The following describes the conditions that forced the massive flight of the Mong.

58   *Mong Resettlement in the United States*

Political Conditions for Mong Massive Flight

On September 14, 1973, a peace accord was signed in Vientiane to end the long political tripartite conflict in Laos. The accord called for a cease fire and for the establishment of a coalition government consisting of the tripartite Cabinet from the Rightists, the Neutralists, and the *Pathet Lao*. Interestingly, the accord emphasized the withdrawal of foreign troops, particularly American and Thai troops, but did not specify the withdrawal of Communist North Vietnamese troops.[1]

Despite the peace agreement, the *Pathet Lao* and the Communist Vietnamese forces continued to attack the positions held by the Mong. On May 6, 1975, General Vang Pao asked *Chao* Souvannaphouma, the head of the coalition government, how to stop the Communist attacks. General Vang Pao was instructed not to fight but only to withdraw. General Vang Pao then resigned from his post as Commander of the Second Military Division of the Royal Lao Army. The author believes that the Mong had been used as a scapegoat by the Lao government for prolonging the tripartite Lao conflict and for delaying the emergence of Laos as a socialist country. The coalition government believed that the reconciliation and healing process within the three Lao factions would occur more rapidly without the presence of the Mong. Souvannaphouma stated later to an official of the French Embassy that:

> The Meo have served me well. Vang Pao has fought well for me. The Meo were good soldiers. What a pity that the price of peace is at their disappearance.[2]

Prince Mangkra Souvannaphouma, son of *Chao* Souvannaphouma and a former colonel in the Lao Air Force, also confirmed this statement:

> He [General Vang Pao] sent message after message to denounce the advance of the Communists. He had the feeling of being abandoned. After the services rendered by his troops and by his Meo people, that was disastrous. As always, the leftist ministers denied this information and accused General Vang Pao of provocation... My father [Souvannaphouma] seemed to accept and believe this version. Nothing will be done to protect the Meo, peace is at this price...[3]

At that time, the communication infrastructure broke down. Rumors that seemed to be true abounded instead. General Vang Pao had no choice but to airlift his families to Udorn, Thailand on May 7, 1975. Two days later, an article was published in the *Khao Xane Pathet Lao*, the official newspaper of the *Neo Lao Hat Sat* (comparable to the newspaper *Pravda* of the Communist party) headed by Souphanouvong. The article stated clearly that "it was necessary to destroy the minority 'Meo' down to the roots."[4]

On May 29, 1975, about 40,000 Mong organized a peaceful march to Vientiane, the capital city, to demand that the coalition government guarantee the security of the people in Xieng Khouang. Two witnesses asserted that upon arrival at the *Hin Heup* area, the multitude was ambushed by the *Pathet Lao* and the Neutralist soldiers. Between 100-140 Mong were either killed or wounded.[5] Official statistics were not available on the numbers of casualties because the throng scattered after the shooting. Those who remained in the area continued to fight the Communists and were named "*Chao-Fa*" (Soldiers of the Sky). They faced excessive military retaliation from the Communist Pathet Lao and Russian aerial attacks with gas rockets of different types. The gassing caused violent headaches, vomiting, diarrhea and death.[6] The Mong referred to the gas as "the Yellow Rain." A Mong leader told Hamilton-Merritt that 20,000 Mong may have been exposed to poisonous gassing during the war. The United States Department of State documented over 13,000 people dead.[7]

In addition, the Mong were persecuted for political reasons. They could either stay behind and be executed as dissidents and political prisoners or flee to Thailand and face an ambiguous future. Approximately 150 Mong families were airlifted to Udorn, Thailand on May 7, 1975. The rest were forced to flee to Thailand on foot. Known as "the Land Refugees," the Mong escaped through jungles, forests, mountains, rivers -- walking for days, months and, in some cases, a year -- before they crossed the Mekong River to reach Thailand. Garrett reflected that there was no place for the Mong to run any more.[8] In Thailand, after they were disarmed and their valuables taken either by the Thai bandits or by the Thai border patrols, they were put into various refugee camps.

Refuge in Thailand

There were two passages through which Mong refugees escaped to Thailand. The first one was through Vientiane and its vicinities across the Mekong River. Those who made their entry through this passage were temporarily put in *Nong Khai* Refugee Camp. The earlier refugees were placed in *Nam Phong* Camp and were later moved to *Ban Vinai* Refugee Camp, which was originally built by the first Mong refugees in 1975. The second passage was by way of the jungle of *Sayaboury* province. Those who made it to Thailand from this route were put into the *Chiang Kham* and *Nam Yao* Refugee Camps in the north. Many other refugee camps in Thailand were also built at the same time for other refugee ethnic groups such as:

Names of the Refugee Camps	Refugee Ethnic Groups
Kapchern Khao I Dang	Cambodian
Napho Phanat Refugee Processing Center (RPC)	Laotian
Nam Yao Ban Vinai Chiang Kham Phanat Nikhom Refugee Processing Center (RPC)	Mong
Bane Thad Phanat Processing	Vietnamese

The numbers of refugees in these camps fluctuated from year to year depending upon how many had been resettled in the West. Thailand received the majority of the refugees from Southeast Asia because its borders are bounded by Laos, Cambodia, Vietnam and Burma (Myanmar). Between 1987 and 1992, the total refugee population in all camps in Thailand averaged over 100,000 a year (See Table 4).

Refugee Registration Process

Each adult refugee was interviewed jointly by Thai government officials and representatives of the United Nations High Commissioner for Refugees (UNHCR). The purpose was to establish their eligibility whether applicants had met the international requirements for refugee status. If they met United Nations' standards, a camp number was issued to the refugee and his or her family. For instance, BV# 1009 stood for *Ban Vinai* case number 1009. If they were not registered by the United Nations and by the Thai government officials, they could be repatriated (sent back to their country of origin). Officials of various countries, such as Canada, Australia, and France occasionally toured the camps to interview and select refugees for resettlement in their countries as well.

The United States based its resettlement selection criteria on family reunification and past employment with the United States government. Refugee adults were normally screened by representatives of the American Council for Voluntary Agencies (ACVA). This ACVA representative was known as "Joint Voluntary Agency" (JVA). Biographical data containing basic information about the case was compiled. Then, the case was referred to the United States Immigration and Naturalization Service officials for interview for admission to the United States.

Table 4. Indochinese Refugee Activity Cumulative Since April 1975, as of December 15, 1991

Countries of Asylum/RPCs	As 9/30/91	91 Arrivals	Since 4/75	To U.S.	3rd Country	Vol. Repartriation	Relocation
Hong Kong	64,138	23,129	215,902	51,625	71,503	10,191	0
Macau	119	3	7,678	2,427	3,868	0	0
Indonesia	19,326	2,293	126,850	42,861	43,058	1,565	0
Malaysai	12,766	379	258,003	89,659	104,843	608	0
Philippines	8,815	359	54,063	10,349	18,929	152	0
Singapore	150	8	35,254	5,709	21,091	5	0
Japan	884	355	4,110	3,047	5,229	0	0
Korea	184	28	393	8	189	0	0
Taiwan	148	0	38	2	35	0	0
Other	0	5	40,856	3,261	28,718	0	0
Thailand-Khmer	14,852	1,612	248,291	50,443	78,604	172	41,172
Thailand-Highlander	49,464	8,308	178,139	53,517	22,026	3,297	0
Thailand-Lao	7,316	847	195,199	72,218	49,031	4,977	1,000
Thailand-Vietnam	14,510	2,749	156,684	37,488	48,341	1,915	0
Subtotal	86,142	13,516	778,313	213,666	198,002	10,361	42,172
Total 1st Asylum	192,672	40,075	1,521,460	422,614	495,456	22,882	42,172
Ref. Processing Center (RPCs)							
Bataan	10,373	1,768	222,921	220,227	6,551	0	12
Galang	0	0	55,501	50,651	4,669	0	0
Phanat Nikhom	2,800	8,902	77,162	74,817	7	0	526
Total RPCs	13,173	10,670	355,584	345,695	11,227	0	538
Viet. to US in 1975	0	--	124,547	123,000	0	1,547	0
Others to US in 1975	0	--	12,000	12,000	0	0	0
Viet. To China in 1977/79	0	--	263,000	0	263,000	0	0
Grand Total	205,845	40,075	1,921,007	903,309	769,683	24,429	42,710

Source: US Department of State, Bureau For Refugee 0Programs, U.S. Committee for Refugees, *Refugee Reports*, Vol. XII, No. 12 (Wasiongton, DC: US Committee for Refugees, 30 December, 1991), 5.

Once a refugee was accepted by the United States government, his or her biographic data was sent to the national Voluntary Agencies (VOLAGs) mostly headquartered in New York and Washington, D.C. In turn, the "bio-data" was sent by the national VOLAGs to their local affiliates, so that local staff could locate the refugee's close relatives or find a local American sponsor.

The VOLAGs receive about $500 per refugee from the United States Department of State. About thirteen prominent national VOLAGs have dominated the initial resettlement of Southeast Asian refugees since 1975. The following illustrates the numbers of refugees resettled by each national VOLAG during the twenty-seven month period from October 1, 1978 to January 1, 1981:

Voluntary Agency	# Resettled
American Council for Nationalities Service (ACNS)	35,216
American Fund for Czechoslovak Refugees (AFCR)	6,771
Buddhist Council for Refugee Rescue and Resettlement	85
Church World Service (CWS)	33,978
Hebrew Immigrant Aid Society (HIAS)	9,265
International Rescue Committee (IRC)	26,737
State of Idaho Program (IDHO)	21
Iowa Refugee Service Center (IRSC)	2,071
Lutheran Immigration and Refugee Services (LIRS)	24,359
Tolstoy Foundation (TF)	4,799
United States Catholic Conference (USCC)	113,974
World Relief Refugee Services (WRRS)	11,437
Young Men's Christian Association (YMCA)	2,313
TOTAL	271,026 [9]

Although the national VOLAGs prepared the arrival paperwork, they passed on the responsibility of the actual resettlement to their local affiliates. It was at the local level where the initial and long-term services of the refugee resettlement process were rendered to each refugee.

Refugee Act of 1980

About 400,000 Southeast Asian refugees were resettled in the United States between 1975-1980 before Congress enacted the Refugee Act of 1980 (PL. 96-212) into law on March 17, 1980. The Act set the overall tone for the resettlement program in the United States and overseas. The goal of the refugee resettlement was "the achievement of self-sufficiency as quickly as possible." A "refugee" was defined broadly as "people subject to persecution in their homeland." The objectives of the Refugee Act of 1980 are:

> to provide a permanent and systematic procedure for the admission to this country of refugees of special humanitarian concern to the United States, and to provide comprehensive and uniform provisions for the effective resettlement and absorption of those refugees who are admitted.[10]

As a result of this act, the policy of the United States toward refugees is to "respond to the urgent needs of persons subject to persecution in their homelands."[11]

In contrast, even though Thailand has been one of the most generous countries towards Southeast Asian refugees, it has maintained a strict policy towards refugees since 1975. Burutphat, a Thai political science professor, indicated, in detail, that Thailand sought to use every means to push refugees out of Thailand's territories. It employed "humane deterrence mechanisms" to control the refugees currently in Thailand to prevent any problems that they might have caused. The humane deterrence mechanisms included the push back policy (refugees are not allowed to enter Thailand, and are pushed back), the confinement of refugees in refugee camps, the disarmament of their weapons, and communication with Laos, Cambodia and Vietnam to repatriate refugees back to their countries. This policy and a standard set of guidelines were approved by the Thai Council of Ministry on June 3, 2518 Buddhist Era (B.E. or 1975). Burutphat asserted that this policy was derived from the trends of various countries. He stated that no country really would want any refugees in their own territory.[12]

Under the Refugee Act of 1980, a US Coordinator for Refugee Affairs was established in the United States Department of State. He or she is responsible for the development of refugee admission and resettlement policy, and coordination of international and domestic refugee resettlement.[13]

The Office of Refugee Resettlement (ORR) was also established in the Act as the administrative body for refugee resettlement in the United States Department of Health and Human Services. ORR was authorized to reimburse cash and medical assistance to state and local governments who provided services to refugees during their resettlement in the United States. Congress appropriated funding through ORR to subcontract with public and private agencies to provide various services to refugees. The services included employment, English language training, health and mental health, education, special education and care/ placement of unaccompanied refugee children.[14]

Statistics for the refugee budgets from 1987-1992 were compiled exclusively for this study. Table 5 and Table 6 provide tabulations for overseas and domestic refugee programs administered through the US Coordinator for Refugee Affairs in the United States Department of State

Table 5. State Department Migration and Refugee Assistance Budget, 1987-1992

	1987 Enacted (1)	1988 Estimated (1)	1989 Request (2)	1990 Request (2)	1991 Request (3)	1992 Request (3)
Refugee Admission Program	108,731,000	119,548,000	115,400,000	231,949,000	185,220	
Refugee Assistance Overseas	194,725,000	176,200,000	197,100,000	168,653	215,220,000	
Other Assistance	34,900,000	34,702,000	19,500,000			
Administration Expenses	8,500,000	8,000,000	8,000,000	8,215,000	8,528,000	10,294,000
Refugee to Israel	N/A	N/A	N/A	29,893,000		
International Organizations	N/A	N/A	N/A	11,036,000		
Total	346,856,000	338,450,000	340,000,000	449,746,000	408,948,000	10,294,000

Compiled by the Author

Source: Department of State, Budget of the U.S. Government:

(1) American Council for Nationalities Services (ACNS), *Refugee Reports*, Vol IX. No. 3 (Washington, DC: ACNS, 18 March 1988), 13.

(2) U.S. Committee for Refugee, *Refugee Reports*, Vol. XI, No. 1 (Washington, DC: U.S. Committee for Refugee, 31 January 6, 1990.

(3) U.S. Committee for Refugees, *Refugee Reports*, Vol. XII, No. 6.

Table 6. ORR Refugee and Entrant Assistance Budgets, 1987 – 1992

	1987 Enacted (1)	1988 Estimated (1)	1989 Actual (2)	1990 Estimated (2)	1991 Actual (3)	1992 Subc. Mark (3)
Cash & Medical Assistance	225,316,000	207,043,000			234,000,000	117,000,000
State-Administered Programs	33,797,000	26,231,000	324,851,000*	285,000,000*	N/A	
Social Services	68,617,000	65,694,000			82,000,000	82,000,000
Employment Services	N/A	N/A	N/A	N/A	N/A	N/A
Voluntary Agencies Matching Grant Programs	3,828,000	7,659,000	15,808,000	40,000,000	40,000,000	40,000,000
Preventative Health	8,039,000	5,840,000	5,770,000	5,770,000	5,700,000	5,700,000
Target Assistance	0	34,466,000	34,052,000	38,052,000	49,000,000	49,000,000
Total	339,597,000	346,933,000	380,481,000	368,822,000	410,700,000	293,700,000

Compiled by the Author.
Source: Office of Refugee Resettlement, Family Support Administration
(1) American Council for Nationalities Service (ACNS), *Refugee Reports*, Vol. IX, No. 2 (Washington, DC: ACNS, 18 March 1988), 13.
(2) U.S. Committee for Refugees, *Refugee Reports*, Vol. XI, No. 1 (Washington, DC: U.S. Committee for Refugees, 31 January 1990), 2.
(3) U.S. Committee for Refugees, *Refugee Reports*, Vol. XII, No. 6 (Washington, DC: U.S. Committee for Refugees, 31 January 1990), 11.
Remark: For 1989-1990, this line item includes cash and medical assistance program, state administration costs, and refugee social services

and through the Office of Refugee Resettlement (ORR), United States Department of Health and Human Services (See Table 5 and Table 6). Similar statistics from budgets from 1975-1986 are not available.

Resettlement by the VOLAGs

VOLAGs is an acronym for the Voluntary Agencies. VOLAGs are not-for-profit entities that engage in resettling refugees in the United States and have identical refugee and program cooperative agreements with the U.S. Department of State.[15] Some national VOLAGs have had their origins dating back to pre-World War II. Their role was to seek admissions of refugees to the United States. For instance, Hebrew Immigrant Aid Society (HIAS) assisted Jews fleeing Nazi persecution.[16] The emergence of the Refugee Relief Act of 1953-54 brought approximately 214,000 refugees from war-torn Europe, and 29,000 "Refugee-Escapees" from Hungary, Korea, Yugoslavia, and China in 1957. In 1959, with the fall of the Batista government in Cuba, an influx of 700,000 Cuban refugees poured into the United States.[17]

In 1975, with the fall of the Cambodian, Lao, and Vietnamese governments to the Communists, the Southeast Asian refugees were brought to the United States for resettlement. With the entry of these refugees, the role of the VOLAGs, that had already focused across the Atlantic, became even more internationalized. Both the national VOLAGs and their local affiliates extended their expertise and resources into a full fledged systematic refugee resettlement process. In fact, the United States government could not have accomplished such a difficult task without the full participation of the VOLAGs. Over a million Southeast Asian refugees and half a million others were resettled in various states by the VOLAGs within a time span of seventeen years since 1975-1992 (See Table 7 for the refugee admissions into the United States by federal fiscal year and Table 8 for the estimated cumulative refugee population by state). The human resources of the VOLAGs have become indispensable to the federal, state, and local governments.

The VOLAGs exemplified the concept of International Non-Governmental Organizations (INGOs) discussed by Boulding. These INGOs were described as:

> the transnational voluntary associations which cover the whole range of human interests and include the chambers of commerce; service clubs; scouting association; YWCAs and YMCAs; churches; and associations of farmers, teachers, doctors, physicists, athletes - any type of groups that seeks relations with people of like interests across national borders., e.g. churches, YMCA, scouting associations.[18]

Table 7. Refugee Admissions into the United States by Federal Fiscal Year

Federal FY	East Asia	East Europe	Soviet Union	Latin America	Africa	Near East & S. Asia	Private Sector	Totals	Admission Ceilings
1975	135,000	1,947	6,211	3,000	0	0		146,158	N/A
1976	15,000	1,756	7,450	3,000	0	0		27,206	N/A
1977	7,000	1,755	8,191	3,000	0	0		19,946	N/A
1978	20,574	2,245	10,688	3,000	0	0		36,507	N/A
1979	76,521	3,393	24,449	7,000	0	0		111,363	N/A
1980	163,799	5,025	28,444	6,662	955	2,231		207,116	N/A
1981	131,139	6,704	13,444	2,017	2,119	3,829		159,252	217,000
1982	73,522	10,780	2,756	602	3,326	6,369		97,355	140,000
1983	39,408	12,083	1,409	668	2,648	5,465		61,681	90,000
1984	51,960	10,285	715	160	2,747	5,246		71,113	72,000
1985	49,970	9,350	640	138	1,953	5,994		68,045	70,000
1986	45,454	8,713	787	173	1,315	5,998		62,440	67,000
1987	40,112	8,606	3,694	315	1,994	10,107		64,828	70,000
1988	35,015	7,818	20,421	2,497	1,588	8,415	733	76,487	87,500
1989	45,680	8,948	39,553	2,605	1,922	6,980	1,550	107,238	116,500
1990	51,611	6,196	50,716	2,309	3,494	4,991	3,009	122,326	125,000
1991	53,485	6,855	38,661	2,237	4,424	5,359	1,789	112,810	131,000
Totals	1,035,250	112,459	258,229	39,383	28,485	70,984	7,081	1,551,87	
1992	52,000	3,000	61,000	3,000	6,000	6,000	10,000		142,000

FFY 1992 has 1,000 unallocated slots assumed in the 142,000 ceiling

Source: Adapted from Refugee Resettlement, U.S. Department of Health and Human Services, U.S. Committee for Refugees, *Refugee Reports*, Vol. XII, No. 12 (Washington, DC: U.S. Committee for Refugees, 30 December 1991), 9.

Table 8. Estimated Cumulative Refugee Population By State*
Including Entries From 1983 through September 1991

State of Residence	Estimated Total	State of Residence	Estimated Total
Alabama	1,800	Nevada	2,700
Alaska	400	New Hampshire	1,500
Arkansas	1,300	New Jersey	13,500
California	229,400	New Mexico	2,000
Colorado	7,300	New York	90,800
Connecticut	8,600	North Carolina	5,700
Delaware	200	North Dakota	1,100
Dist. of Columbia	4,400	Ohio	10,500
Florida	27,300	Oklahoma	3,900
Georgia	11,400	Oregon	11,400
Hawaii	2,500	Pennsylvania	21,700
Idaho	2,500	Rhode Island	4,200
Illinois	29,600	South Carolina	800
Indiana	2,400	Tennessee	1,400
Iowa	5,500	Texas	6,100
Kansas	5,100	Utah	5,900
Kentucky	2,900	Vermont	1,000
Louisiana	5,400	Virginia	14,500
Maine	2,300	Washington	25,500
Maryland	12,500	West Virginia	9,700
Massachussetts	26,400	Wisconsin	100
Michigan	12,800	Guam	100
Minnesota	18,900	*Other territories	100
Mississippi	900	Puerto Rico	100
Missouri	8,600		
Montana	500	TOTAL	706,700
Nebraska	2,200		

*Estimates include all major populations. Adjustments for secondary
migration through FY 1990. All totals rounded to the nearest hundred.
Source: Adapted from Office of Refugee Resettlement, U.S.
Department of Health and Human Services. U.S. Committee for
Refugees, *Refugee Reports*, Vol. XII, No. 12 (Washington, DC: U.S.
Committee for Refugees, 30 December 1991), 9.

Boulding estimated that over 102 non-aligned countries affiliated with neither the United States nor the Soviet Union and 18,000 active non-governmental organizations existed in the world in 1985-1986. If these countries and organizations were all active as VOLAGs and if all these resources were brought "to the table," a new civic order as foreseen by Boulding might emerge. According to Boulding, this substantive demographic, political, organizational base can build a new civic order for the world without violence through "peace education." She sketched a metaphysics of civics and introduced the notion of social imagination by giving civics a new meaning. History and the future were seen as an expanded sense of the present of a span over two hundred years.[19]

Refugee resettlement is an example of a project and process involved based on involvement of "grassroots." Such projects were more locally determined, e.g. agency to people, people to people. This integration of community-based involvement from the bottom up was known as the grassroots/integrated-community based approach.

Southeast Asian Refugees

The Southeast Asian refugees mainly came from Cambodia, Laos, and Vietnam. In the past, two terms were widely used: Indochinese and Southeast Asian refugees. Many refugees from Cambodia, Laos, and Vietnam do not want to be called "Indochinese refugee." Historically, the French lumped Cambodia, Laos, and Vietnam into "French Indochina." Therefore, the term "Indochinese refugees" implies that they are still under the French protectorate, which is no longer true. Because the term "Indochinese refugee" has a negative connotation dating back to French Indochina, "Southeast Asian refugee" will be used instead.

Even though all Southeast Asian refugees may look similar to many Westerner observers, there are at least six major groups. These groups are completely distinct in their language, religion, history, and culture. From Cambodia are the Cambodians and the Chinese-Cambodians. From Laos are the Lao and the Mong. From Vietnam are the Vietnamese, the Chinese-Vietnamese and the montagnards. In addition to the Lao and the Mong, there were other ethnic groups of refugees from Laos. These include the *Iu Mien* (or the *Yao*), *Khamu, Lahu, Lao Theung,* and *Lao Lue.* Since the numbers of these groups are not substantial, the author will not cover them in any detail. However, for statistical purposes, the numbers of the Iu Mien, the Mong, and the other ethnic groups were recorded as one broad group from the country of nationality (See Table 9 - for the Southeast Asian Refugee Arrivals in the United States by Nationality, FY 75-93). In Table 9, a new group of refugees was introduced. They are the Amerasians. The term

"Amerasians" refers to children born out of wedlock of Southeast Asian women and American soldiers who were deployed to Southeast Asia during the Vietnam Conflict.

Table 9 - Southeast Asian Arrivals by Nationality, FY 1975 - FY 1993

By Nationality	Numbers
Amerasians	67,233
Cambodia	146,328
Laos	225,675
Vietnam	632,713
Total	1,072,471

Source: Adapted from Office of Refugee Resettlement, *Report to the Congress FY 1993: Refugee Resettlement Program* (Washington, D.C.: U.S. Department of Health and Human Services, Administration for Children and Families, 1993), A2-A3.

Amerasians have also been called 'the children of dust.' Between 1975-1993, 67,233 Amerasians, 146,328 Cambodians, 225,675 Laotians, and 632,713 Vietnamese were resettled in the United States. The numbers totaled to 1,072,471 in 1993.

These refugee groups from Laos, Cambodia, and Vietnam, similar to the Mong, were forced out of Southeast Asia since 1975 and have been resettled in various states throughout the United States. These groups consist of the Cambodians, the Lao, the Vietnamese, and the Chinese from Southeast Asia. The following paragraphs describe a brief historical and cultural background of the major Southeast Asian refugee groups in the United States.

The Cambodians

The *Cambodians* were a mixture of tribesmen of either Indonesian origin or Indian, Javanese, and Chinese descent. Their history dated back to the 5th century when they inhabited Cambodia. Cambodia was colonized by the French and became independent in the 1950's under King Sihanouk. The Cambodians are Buddhists, family-oriented, and artistic. The society was divided into several layers of hierarchical social classes reflecting its monarchy system and religion. Cambodians are often described as shy, humble, submissive, and easy going but frank and honest in their opinions and feelings. King Sihanouk was overthrown by General Lon Nol in the 1970's through U.S. involvement to wipe out the Communists at the Cambodian borders.[20] When the Communists took over Cambodia, Pol Pot massacred over three million Cambodians. This was a tragic holocaust in Asia illustrated by the film "*The Killing Fields*."[21]

The Lao

The *Lao* were related to the Northern Thai sharing their Sino-Indian cultural traditions and Buddhism. The Chinese mentioned their existence around the Yangtze Kiang River before 800 BC. The Lao established the Kingdom of *Lan Xang* (the "Land of a Million Elephants") in 1353 AD. They value flexibility, adaptability, harmony, interpersonal relations, autonomy, and a gentle life style. Like the Cambodians, the Lao society was also divided into several layers of hierarchical social classes influenced by its monarchy and religion. Laos was colonized by the French in the early nineteenth century, gained its independence after World War II, and established a constitutional monarchy. However, the tripartite civil war emerged and grew as part of the Vietnam conflict.[22] The Communists took control over Laos in 1975 after the United States withdrew its troops from Southeast Asia.

The Vietnamese

The *Vietnamese* were under Chinese rule until the tenth century. Vietnam was torn by internal political strife and was divided along the seventeenth parallel during the seventeenth century. The *Trinh's* ruled in the North and the *Nguyen's* in the South. Vietnam was colonized by the French in 1884. *Ho Chi Minh* declared independence in 1946 and won the battle over the French at *Dien Bien Phu*. The Geneva Convention of 1954 officially divided Vietnam at the seventeenth parallel: North Vietnam under *Ho Chi Minh* and South Vietnam under *Bao Dai* and later *Ngo Dinh Diem*. The Vietnam conflict became more intensified when the United States became involved in the 1960's. Its culture is more Chinese-like and different from its neighboring countries. Though Buddhism plays a major role in the Vietnamese society, Confucianism influenced many Vietnamese. Confucianism stresses the importance of applied politics of correct social comportment and political relationship.[23] Through French influence, many Vietnamese were converted to Catholicism. Since 1975, the term 'Boat People' has been widely used to refer to the Vietnamese refugees who escaped from Vietnam on boats on the high seas.

The Chinese from Vietnam

The Chinese from Southeast Asia comprised a sizable population in Laos, Cambodia, and Vietnam. This following paragraph describes a brief historical and cultural background of the Chinese-Vietnamese from

Vietnam. Since they focused mainly on economic development, they controlled many commercial and industrial enterprises in Southeast Asia. Koschmann divided ethnic Chinese from Southeast Asia into three groups: the *Ming Huong*, the Cantonese, and the Taiwanese. The Minh Huong migrated from China to Vietnam during the Ming Dynasty (1368-1644). They are a part of the Vietnamese. The Cantonese, who left China during the Ch'ing Dynasty (1644-1911), accounted for the majority of the Chinese in Southeast Asia. The Taiwanese with strong political ties to Taiwan moved to Vietnam in the 1950's. They encouraged an anti-Communist sentiment among the Chinese population in Vietnam. After the fall of Saigon, the Communists began implementing a policy of shifting the Chinese to different economic zones. They attacked Cholon where most of the Chinese were concentrated. That signaled the beginning of Communist genocide against the ethnic Chinese.[24]

Mong Refugees in the United States

The Mong were brought to the United States like other Southeast Asian refugees. After passing an interview with the Immigration and Naturalization Service officers, Mong refugees were referred to the International Committee on Migration (ICM) for physical examinations and for travel arrangements. Then, they were transported from the refugee camps to Phanat Nikhom Transit camp in Bangkok, Thailand to travel to the United States. The transportation costs were loans to them that they must repay to the government through their sponsoring agencies at a later date.

The first Mong refugees who arrived in the United States in 1975 were General Vang Pao and his families. They were sponsored by one of the national VOLAGs in conjunction with local churches and private American sponsors in Missoula, Montana. Reder reports resettlement counts of Lao hill tribes (Highland Lao in which the Mong were also included) in the United States by year of entry. In 1975, the Lao hill tribes only accounted for 301 people.[25] North found that most of the refugees who left in 1975 were urban elite, well-educated, and often speaking French or English. More Mong were brought to various states across the United States in the following years. The peak of the Mong arrivals was in 1980 when 27,242 came to the United States.[26]

The exact counts of Mong were uncertain because they were a subgroup of the Highland Lao and the Highland Lao a subgroup of the Lao; therefore, Mong were not always counted separately. Most of the statistics were kept by country of nationality instead of ethnic identity. Table 10 contains the best estimates provided by Reder during 1975-1980 [27] and by Yang and North during 1981-1988.[28] The counts were consolidated to bring the numbers up to 1988. (See Table 10 for the

Table 10. Highland Lao Arrivals in the United States, FY 75-88

Federal Fiscal Year	Arrivals
1975	301
1976	3,056
1977	1,655
1978	3,873
1979	11,301
1980	27,242
1981	6,039
1982	2,600
1983	738
1984	2,753
1985	1,944
1986	3,668
1987	8,307
1988	10,388
Total	83,865

Compiled by the Author.
Source: Adapted from Stephen Reder, The Hmong Resettlement Study, Vol. 1, Final Report (Washington, DC: U.S. Department of Health and Human Services, 1985), 2:36; and
Doua Yang and David S. North, *Profiles of the Highland Lao Communities in the United States* (Washington, DC: U.S. Department of Health and Human Services, 1988), 7.

Highland Lao Arrivals in the United States, Fiscal Year 1975-1988). However, the majority of the Highland Lao are Mong regardless of the counts.

In Yang and North's study in 1988, the Mong were distributed in seventy-one communities in thirty states. The estimated Mong population nationwide totaled over 105,253 including US births (see Table 11 for the estimated Cumulative Mong Refugee Population by State). Other Highland Lao (Iu Mien, Khmu or Lao Theung, Lahu, Lao Lue) were found in nineteen communities and accounted for over 12,700 (See Table 12 for the estimated non-Mong Highland Lao Population by State through November 1988).[29] Yang and North's report reflected a national picture of the status of Highland Lao resettlement as of 1988. It was notable that eighty-five percent of the Mong lived in three states: fifty-six percent in California, sixteen percent in Wisconsin, and thirteen percent in Minnesota. In 1988, the largest Mong concentrations in the United States were Fresno, California with 24,000; St. Paul, Minnesota with 13,450; and Merced, California with 7,500. The following describes some of the adjustment difficulties of the Mong.

Adjustment Problems of the Mong in the United States

The early Mong refugees were more educated and more comfortable with western culture than later arrivals (as was true with the rest of the Southeast Asian refugees). They had less problems with the adjustment to the mainstream of American culture. In contrast, those who arrived after 1978 constituted the majority of the Mong and spoke neither English nor French like their early counterparts. Many experienced culture shock. Immediately upon their arrival, they were exposed to American family life and customs. Some of the common symptoms of culture shock include disorientation of time, anxiety and withdrawal, fear of coping with the new daily tasks and the new environment, such as living in the high-rise building, nervousness, unusual fatigue, and suspicion towards the members of the new culture. Koschmann and Tobin defined "culture shock" as:

> a phenomenon when one finds himself/herself in the middle of a new culture in which cues are difficult or impossible to interpret which produces feelings of disorientation, inadequacy, and isolation.[30]

Almost all of the refugees experienced some form of culture shock. Some expressed this shock through depression and crying. The effects of culture shock were increased when refugees obtained information only through an interpreter. Some refugees displayed psychosomatic symptoms such as recurring headaches and digestion problems.

Table 11. Estimated Mong Refugee Population By State Through
November 1988

State of Residence	Estimated Total	State of Residence	Estimated Total
Arkansas	46	New York	300
California	58,976	North Carolina	818
Colorado	1,300	Ohio	455
Connecticut	300	Oklahoma	455
Georgia	823	Oregon	1,130
Illinois	702	Pennsylvania	750
Indiana	65	Rhode Island	2,178
Iowa	403	South Carolina	84
Kansas	600	South Dakota	22
Massachussetts	525	Tennessee	105
Michigan	2,610	Texas	395
Minnesota	13,700	Utah	168
Montana	390	Virginia	34
Nebraska	366	Washington	1,182
New Jersey	70	Wisconsin	16,456
		Total	105,253

Estimates include all Mong population. Adjustments for secondary
migration through FY 1988

Compiled by the Author.

Source: Adapted from Survey of Mong Community leaders by CZA,
Inc. by Doua Yang and David S. North, *Profiles of the Highland Lao
Communities in the United States* (Washington, DC: US Department of
Health and Human Services, 1988), 10-12.

Table 12. Estimated Non-Mong Highland Lao Population By State Through November 1988

State of Residence	Estimated Total	State of Residence	Estimated Total
Ethnic Iu Mien		Ethnic Lahu	
Alaska	65	California	391
California	8,032	Minnesota	45
Oregon	1,500	Subtotal	436
Washington	756		
Subtotal	10,288	Ethnic Lao Theung	
		Minnesota	220
Ethnic Khamu			
California	1,200		
Massachussets	70		
Oklahoma	117	Ethnic Lao Lue	
Texas	70	Texas	120
Washington	256		
Subtotal	1,713	Total	12,777

*Estimates include all Non-Mong Highland Lao population.
Adjustment for secondary migration through FY 1988.

Compiled by the Author.

Source: Adapted from Survey of Mong Community Leaders by CZA, Inc.
Doua Yang and David S. North, Profiles of the Highland Lao Communities in the United States (Washington, DC: US Department of Health and Human Services, 1988), 13-1.

Some would express desperation since they needed to learn the most basic common daily tasks taken for granted by a typical American. Many reported anxiety resulting from activities such as shopping for groceries, using public transportation, acclimating to different climates, coping with standards of personal and public safety, reacting to emergency situations, and learning to read street signs. These daily tasks might look simple to Americans, but to Mong refugees, learning many things in a short period of time was overwhelming.

In addition, Mong were resettled far from one another and found themselves alienated. In such isolation, learning simple daily tasks could be very stressful. Their earlier experience as guerrilla fighters and rice farmers and housewives were not considered transferable skills in the new land.

Between 1981-1982, a unique problem emerged among the Mong refugees. They began to move to Orange County, California in massive numbers. This phenomenon was known as "secondary migration," in which refugees moved from the first place of resettlement to a new location to reunify either with their relatives or for other reasons.

As a result of this secondary migration, Indochina Refugee Action Center (IRAC) in Washington, D.C. sponsored a national conference for about thirty Mong and other Highland Lao representatives to meet with top federal refugee program officials on February 3-4, 1983. The objectives were to discuss the key problems Mong refugees faced, and to find a bipartisan solution to the problems. Ambassador Eugene Douglas (U.S. Coordinator for Refugee Affairs, U.S. Department of State), Mr. James N. Purcell, Jr. (Director of Bureau for Refugee Programs, U.S. Department of State), and Dr. Phillips Hawkes (Director of the Office of Refugee Resettlement, U.S. Department of Health and Human Services) were present at the conference. Secondary migration was highlighted as a major problem for the U.S. Department of State, the Office of Refugee Resettlement, and for the Mong. When the Mong refugees moved from their initial place of resettlement to a new location, they moved by the hundreds. Therefore, secondary migration did not only affect the local and state programs in the initial resettlement sites but impacted those ones in the secondary resettlement sites as well. As a Mong representative from Illinois and spokesman at the conference, the author presented secondary migration as the most pressing problem for Mong refugees in the nation. Secondary migration posed a major concern for the Mong representatives because still more Mong were planning to move to California.

In order to prevent such an urgent problem from recurring, four suggestions were presented to the top federal officials for consideration:

1. The United States government should make funding available to
    Mong Mutual Assistance Associations (MAAs) across the United
    States to conduct extensive workshops and orientation sessions to
    Mong communities in the targeted areas and to receive newcomers
    from other states.
2. The United States government should provide technical assistance,
    develop agribusiness and other economic development projects to
    targeted Mong communities.
3. The United States government should assist Mong refugees to
    establish a clearinghouse network consisting of a steering
    committee of the Mong Mutual Assistance Associations (MAAs)
    in the targeted Mong communities.
4. The federal, state, and local governments should pay greater
    attention to the fundamental needs of the Mong communities. The
    Mong demonstrated that they needed special assistance to cope
    with their basic needs.

Ambassador Douglas acknowledged the fact that the United States
Department of State had neglected the Highland Lao refugees in the
past.   Evidenced by the massive movement of Mong secondary
migration across the United States, Douglas advised the highland Lao
representatives to inform the refugees to start making concrete plans for
future and permanent settlement in the United States. In turn, Douglas
established a position in his office and asked the Office of Refugee
Resettlement (ORR) and each Governor to take steps to respond to the
Highland Lao's needs. During the course of the conference, an in-depth
assessment of the cause of Mong secondary migration was assembled
by the representatives. They concurred that several factors could have
contributed to the cause of Mong secondary migration across the
nation. The following paragraphs describe those factors.

Lack of Knowledge and Access to Jobs

Employment difficulties were the most pressing problems for Mong
refugees. The problem of finding jobs was interwoven and interrelated
with other complex problems such as language barriers, lack of
marketable skills as required by employers, service-cuts, poor health,
lack of economic development and discrimination in hiring practices.

Family Reunification

The Mong cultural tradition emphasizes an extended family and clan
orientation. Consequently, the members of the same clan tended to
cluster in specific cities or states. The purpose was to create a support
system to provide mutual assistance to one another socially,

politically, and educationally. Though the Mong were resettled in various states beginning in 1978, they started a movement to cluster in particular cities such as St. Paul, Fresno, Merced, Stockton, Portland, Philadelphia, Chicago, Green Bay, etc.

Service-Cuts

Service cuts were identified as one of the causes of secondary migration. Beginning around 1982, the federal government applied a policy of an eighteen-month cut off of Refugee Cash Assistance (RCA). The Mong could not find jobs prior to the completion of the eighteenth month in the United States. In addition, their low level of cultural adaptation made it exceedingly difficult for them to cope with the modern systems such as General Assistance job search policies. Since they could not find jobs in a timely manner and since services were cut, moving to other localities appeared to many to be the way out.

Unequal Distribution of Services

The distribution of services between counties and states was uneven. One state may provide better services to refugees than another. For instance, California, Minnesota, and Wisconsin provide more opportunities to refugees to have access to educational (especially vocational) services than Ohio and Illinois. It was typical for refugees to shop around for opportunities in education, career training and English language training.

Sudden Unexplained Death Syndrome (SUDS)

Cultural shock continues to linger for some Mong. Closely related to the issue of cultural shock, Mong experienced an unusual phenomenon for Mong males. This is referred by the Mong as "*Tuag tsaugzug*" [Sleeping Death] or what experts termed "Sudden Unexplained Death Syndrome." (SUDS) is a striking and horrified phenomenon associated with the migration and the Mong during their transition to become Mong-Americans in the United States. Sherman reported that about 115 Mong in the United States had died mysteriously in their sleep.[31] The author estimated that over 200 Mong males between the age of twenty and fifty-five may have died from the SUDS phenomenon. Munger described the characteristic moaning, choking, and snoring sounds at the time of death among the twenty documented cases. However, there was no record of Mong having died in their sleep in Laos.

There were similarities between the Mong and their Sudden Unexplained Death Syndrome and the "*bangungut*" ("Oriental nightmare death syndrome") experienced by Filipino males in Hawaii in Oahu County from 1937 to 1948.[32] Doctors have long recognized this phenomenon, but have been unable to explain the fatal cause that frightens the sleeping Filipino males to death. Aponte stated that Filipino healthy males were said to die during the night making moaning, snoring, or choking noises as well.[33] Oalmann specified that "the interval between the onset of symptoms and the death is less than twenty-four hours."[34] Though several experts linked sudden death syndrome to nightmare fright due to stress of cultural assimilation,[35] chemical exposure during the warfare in Laos,[36] or congenital effects due to inbreeding,[37] there is no sufficient evidence to support these claims. Why did sudden death happen to the Mong in the United States? The answer still remains a mystery.

In 1983, the author personally witnessed two Mong males who died in Chicago as a result of this SUDS phenomenon. A fifty-year old Mong man, Nao Soua Thao, who appeared perfectly healthy, arrived in Chicago in July and died in his sleep two months after arriving in the United States. In December of the same year, Nao Soua Thao's twenty-year old son, Blong Thao, who also seemed perfectly healthy, came to reunify with the rest of his families in Chicago. Two weeks after his arrival in Chicago, he also died in his sleep. The autopsy of these two men could not reveal the cause of their death.

Vocational Adjustment and Gender Role Adjustment

Like any other refugees, the Mong went through a period of vocational adjustment and sex role adjustment.[38] In Laos, one's professional and vocational status was intertwined with his identity, social respect, and self-esteem. In the United States, adjustment in the new culture meant an adjustment to a new self identity. Many former high ranking military officials who were illiterate had difficulty coping with vocational adjustment by accepting minimal paying jobs such as custodians. Many Mong males also experienced the evolving sex role adjustment. Men were traditionally the breadwinners for the families. However, this was no longer true in the United States. Circumstances required two incomes to support a family. They resented the economic independence of their wives and were threatened by the sexually integrated work force.

Highland Lao Initiatives (HLI)

Because the Mong demonstrated that they needed special assistance, the Office of Refugee Resettlement (ORR), U.S. Department of Health and Human Services (DHHS) initiated approximately $3 millions in emergency funds, called the "Highland Lao Initiative" (HLI), to assist

34,500 Mong and other Highland Lao outside of California and Minnesota. The funding was equally distributed on a non-competitive basis to the counties impacted by Mong refugees. This mechanism was aimed at keeping Mong intact in their existing communities and to prevent secondary migration to the Central Valley of California. North summarized that the objectives of the Highland Lao Initiative (HLI) were primarily intended to increase employment, decrease welfare dependency, stabilize the Highland Lao communities and stem secondary migration, particularly to the Central Valley of California.[39]

By 1983, ORR funded forty-seven programs in the nation in areas where Mong were concentrated. In the following year, ORR contracted with Coffey, Zimmerman and Associates, Inc. of Washington, DC to conduct an evaluation of thirty-two of the forty-seven programs funded by HLI to determine their effects. (The author was among the six member team selected to evaluate this project). The HLI programs were funded to deliver eight categories of services: outreach, job placement, on-the-job training (OJT), vocational training, craft development, English as a Second Language (ESL), farm and garden, other business development and day-care.[40] Of the thirty-two programs which offered direct employment services, fourteen were evaluated. Two hundred eighty-six people secured employment through HLI.[41] Seven programs used the OJT technique that resulted in seventy-one job placements.[42] Portland, Toledo, and Omaha employed the vocational training approach. In Portland, 186 Mong signed up for the classes and 112 were placed in jobs. In Toledo, forty-four refugees received training and fourteen secured employment. In Omaha, a Mong store was established for store operation training. Fifty-two refugees enrolled in the program and eight were upgraded into better positions. Other programs were in the process of evaluation. Some of the projects could not be evaluated in terms of cost effectiveness.[43]

The emergence of the Highland Lao Initiative (HLI) as a one time aid in 1983 provided by the federal government temporarily stabilized the Mong communities outside of California and Minnesota. It encouraged some hope in the Mong communities that the federal government cared about them. HLI seems to have slowed down Mong secondary migration to a certain extent as reflected in Yang and North's data collection. In 1988, Yang and North reported that 58,976 Mong lived in California (fifty-six percent), 16,456 in Wisconsin (sixteen percent), 13,700 in Minnesota (thirteen percent), and 16,121 Mong scattered in twenty-seven other states (fifteen percent).[44] In comparison, the total Mong population in 1984 outside of California and Minnesota was 31,966;[45] whereas in 1988 it remained steady at 32,577.[46]

Summary

When the Communists took over Laos in 1975, the Mong had to seek asylum in Thailand. As allies of the United States, the Mong were persecuted for political reasons. Some of these Mong refugees were brought to the United States for resettlement. Chapter 4 examined the Mong resettlement in the United States. By coming from a predominantly rural, and preliterate background with few transferable marketable skills, the Mong had difficulties in adjustment to the new culture. The adjustment problems resulted in massive secondary migration to various states, particularly the Central Valley of California. The problems of the Mong tend to center around the lack of knowledge and access to jobs in order to achieve self-economic sufficiency, the need for family reunification, the federal policy on service cuts, the unequal distribution of services in various states, the horrible phenomenon of "Sudden Unexplained Death Syndrome" (SUDS), the struggle for reestablishment of self-identity and the vocational adjustment.

Chapter 5 will provide a critical and analytical retrospection on the formal educational system in Laos in comparison to the United States'. The discussion will include an in-depth analysis of the numerous social and educational problems that Mong-American students have faced. The author will provide some suggestions on how to remedy these problems.

Notes

[1]Prince Mangkra Souvannaphouma, *L'Agonie du Laos* (Plon: Presse de la Simped, 1975), 2:36.
[2]Jean Larteguy, *La Fabuleuse Aventure du Peuple de l'Opium* (Paris: Presses de la Cite, 1979), 14:236-238.
[3]Souvannaphouma, 101.
[4]Larteguy, 14:243.
[5]Ibid., 14:243-250.
[6]Ibid., 253.
[7]Jane Hamilton-Merritt, "Tragic Legacy from Laos", *The Reader's Digest*, August 1981, 96-100.
[8]W.E. Garrett, "The Hmong of Laos: No Place to Run," *National Geographic*, Vol. 145, No. 1 (Washington, D.C.: National Geographic Society, January 1974),78-111.
[9]United States Committee for Refugees, *1981 World Refugee Survey* (Washington, D.C.: United States Committee for Refugees, 1981), 19.
[10]U.S. Congress, House, Committee on the Judiciary, *Immigration and Nationality Acts*, H.R. 101st Congress, 1st session (Washington, D.C.: U.S. Government Printing Office, 1989), 313-316.
[11]Ibid., 313.

[12]Khachaphay Buruphat, *Chone Kloum Noi Nai Thai Kup Khouame Mane Khong Khaun Chat* [Minorities in Thailand and National Security] (Bangkok: Praie Pittaya Publishing, Co., B.E. 2526 [1983]), 277-315.
[13]*Immigration and Nationality Act*, 315.
[14]Ibid., 316.
[15]David S. North, Lawrence S. Lewin, and Jennifer R. Wagner, *Kaleidoscope: The Resettlement of Refugees in the U.S. by the Voluntary Agencies* (Washington, D.C.: New TransCentury Foundation, Lewin and Associates, and National Opinion Research Center, 1982), 26.
[16]David S. North et al, *An Evaluation of the Highland Lao Initiative* (Washington, D.C.: Office of Refugee Resettlement, U.S. Department of Health and Human Services, 1985), 19.
[17]*Immigration and Nationality Act*, 422-423.
[18]Elise Boulding, *Building a Global Civic Culture: Education for an Interdependent World* (New York: Teachers College Press, 1988), 3:35.
[19]Ibid., 3:35 and 7:138.
[20]Nancy Lee Koschmann and Joseph Jay Tobin, *Working with Indochinese Refugees: A Handbook for Mental Health and Human Service Providers* (Chicago: Travelers Aid/ Immigrants' Service League of Chicago, n.d.), 15-17.
[21]Frank N. Magill, *Magill's Cinema Annual 1985: A Survey of 1984 Films* (Englewood, NJ: Salem Press, 1985), 270-276.
[22]Koschmann and Tobin, 18-19.
[23]Ibid., 22-25.
[24]Ibid., 26-27.
[25]Stephen Reder, *The Hmong Resettlement Study*, Final Report, Vol. 1 (Washington, D.C.: U.S. Department of Health and Human Services, 1985), 2:36.
[26]David S. North et al, *Kaleidoscope: The Resettlement of Refugees in the U.S. by the Voluntary Agencies* (Washington, D.C.: New TransCentury Foundation, Lewin and Associates, and National Opinion Research Center, 1982), 5.
[27]Reder, 36.
[28] Doua Yang and David S. North, *Profiles of the Highland Lao Communities in the United States* (Washington, D.C.: U.S. Department of Health and Human Services, 1988), 7.
[29]Ibid., 32-125.
[30]Koschmann and Tobin, 4.
[31]Spencer Sherman, "The Hmong in America: Laotian Refugees in the 'Land of the Giants'", *National Geographic*, Vol. 174, No. 4. (Washington, DC: National Geographic Society, October 1988), 587-610.
[32]Ronald G. Munger, "Sudden Adult Death in Asian Population: The Case of the Hmong", *The Hmong in the West*, ed. (Minneapolis: University of Minnesota, 1982), 301 and 308-310.
[33]G.D. Aponte, "The Enigma of Bangungut", *Annals of Internal Medicine*, 52: 1258-1263.
[34]M.C. Oalmann et al, "Sudden Death, Coronary Heart Disease,

Atherosclerosis and Myocardial Lesion in Young Men", *American Journal of Epidemiology*, 112 (5): 308-310.
[35]Joseph Westermeyer, "Hmong Deaths", *Science*, Vol. 213. 1982, 952.
[36]Bruce Thowpaou Bliatout, *Hmong Sudden Unexpected Nocturnal Death Syndrome: A Cultural Study* (Portland, Oregon: Sparkle Publishing Enterprises, Inc., 1982), 45-47.
[37]Eliot Marshall, "The Hmong: Dying of Culture Shock?", *Science*, Vol. 12, 1981, 22-23.
[38]Koschmann and Tobin, 7-8.
[39]David S. North et al, iv.
[40]Ibid., 28.
[41]Ibid., 44-50.
[42]Ibid., 51-56.
[43]Ibid., 56-60.
[44]Yang and North, 9.
[45]North et al, 8.
[46]Yang and North, 9.

Chapter 5

Mong Education at the Crossroads

This chapter will provide a critical analysis of the formal education system in Laos in relation to that of the United States. The discussion will describe the numerous social and educational problems that Mong students have encountered. The case of Toua, a prototypic Mong-American case, will be used throughout this chapter to illustrate the themes of this chapter. All the names of the individuals and places in this chapter are fictitious to safeguard the confidentiality of the subject-participants involved in the study. The author also adheres strictly to the policies and procedures of the Institutional Review Board (IRB). The themes personified by the case involved a real life experience as experienced by the case to reflect some of the most challenging adjustment problems during his initial resettlement as a refugee who lived through the transition period of resettlement in a new country. Then, the author will offer some recommendations on how to remedy this situation.

The Mong people as a group are going through a period of sporadic changes since migrating unexpectedly from Laos through Thailand to the United States. They have experienced tremendous changes in almost every aspect of their lives. They are forced to change their way of life and to adjust and adapt quickly to the social norms of the new society. Their acquisition of knowledge needs to be accelerated at an unprecedented rate as they begin their new lives in the "Information Age" in the highly technological US society.

As the Mong make some abrupt changes in their lives, they are faced with some of the most crucial social and educational problems during their adjustment from Mong to Mong-Americans. Their experiences reflect the old American saying: "No pain, No gain." Thao's study found that the Mong refugees who came to the Chicago area between 1978 and 1987 experienced tremendous frustration.[vi] This frustration was due to numerous problems including adjustment to the new educational system; loss of native language and culture; development of intergenerational gaps between parents and children; confusion due to cultural differences, diversity, and conformity; "Over-Americanization;" issues related to gangs; role shifts between parents and children; misconceptions about the role of teachers; concerns about morality and the transmission of social values; lack of prior knowledge and similar experience that can be passed on to their children; and a feeling of frustration from not being able to help their children develop to their full potential. The next few paragraphs describe each of these problems.

1. Adjustment to the New Educational System

When we thoroughly examine the two educational systems in Laos versus the United States, a clear distinction is evident. The Mong, to a certain extent, have been influenced by the French educational system. From history, the French colonization brought the entry of the European model to Laos including its educational system that was implemented in Laos for nearly fifty years from 1892-1947. This system was highly centralized, traditional, national, and teacher-centered. This was a top-down approach and its goal of education was mainly to prepare bilingual interpreters and functionaries to carry out the functions of the French. The method of instruction emphasized heavily rote memorization with strong discipline and corporal punishment.

In contrast, the educational system in the United States utilizes an integrated community-based approach. This model is a combination of local control, centralization, decentralization, modernity and student-center using various methods of instruction. The goal of the American education system is to teach young people to think things out for themselves. Therefore, students are encouraged to ask questions when they do not understand. One of the objectives of schooling is to prepare them to be good workers in the future.[2] A case example will illustrate the differences between the process of educational system in Laos and in the United States as experienced by Toua.

Toua was eleven years old when his family came to Chicago in 1982. Toua could remember vividly that he went to half a year first grade in Laos prior to arriving in the Vinai Refugee Camp,

Thailand. His family stayed in the refugee camp in Thailand from 1976-1982. During that six-year period in the refugee camp, Toua had the opportunity to learn how to read and write Thai and some basic English, so he could only speak a few words of English. After Toua and his family were settled in an apartment on the North side of the City of Chicago, his refugee resettlement worker enrolled him in James Elementary School. Toua could not understand why he was placed in the sixth grade when he could only speak a few words of English. If he were back in Laos, Toua could have been placed in the first grade. His teacher would have written his lessons on the board and would have required him to recite his lessons *par-coeur* (memorize by heart) on a daily basis. If he could not memorize his lessons by heart, he could have been punished by standing in the corner of the classroom for hours. His teacher could have called his parents and reported Toua's failings to them.

At James Elementary School, Toua was pulled out of class to work with his English as a Second Language (ESL) teacher and then returned back to his homeroom teacher, Mrs. Gilfillian. His teacher used a lot of pictures and he was told to repeat after her and she interwove her lessons with exercises to reinforce what she taught. Every day when Toua came to class, she did not even require him to recite his lessons *par-coeur* (memorize by heart) like in Laos. He started to enjoy the new activities that she presented in class. Every day there was always something new in terms of activities. Toua did not have to be embarrassed by standing in the corner of the classroom any more. He did not have to worry about his answers because he knew that she would not punish him if he gave the wrong answers. She was willing to work with him even more and encouraged him that he had made a lot of progress. Toua did not have to worry about his parents now because she could not speak Mong and could not communicate in Mong with his parents anyway. All he knew was that she had not beaten any students in her classes before. However, he was surprised to see many of his classmates talking back to her. Back in Laos, if he talked back to his teacher like them, he could have been in a deep trouble. He could have been suspended for a few days. Well! It was different in the United States. Toua did not quite understand how the educational system worked yet and he would have to learn more. Besides attending the special class, Toua remained with Mrs. Gilfillian in the same classroom for the whole year.

2. Language Barrier

The language barrier continues to impact the rate of adjustment for the Mong at all levels. Educationally, Mong parents and children have experienced difficulties in adjustment. From kindergarten to high school levels, Mong students needed to adjust to the language barrier, the pressure of becoming academically proficient in the content areas, and peer pressure. Besides being overwhelmed by their daily tasks, some Mong students' English language proficiency levels were so limited that they could not be placed into the mainstream classrooms.

To continue Toua's story, in 1983, Toua was promoted to the Joan Middle School. The environment was quite different from James Elementary School. Though some things were quite similar to James Elementary School, his classmates were taller than him. They started to call him, I quote "Chinese! Chinese!" and "Jap!" and "Hey! Chink!" Toua did not quite understand what those terms meant. In addition, some American students came to challenge Toua to a fist fight. They thought that Toua knew kick-boxing and martial arts. Because Toua refused to fight them, they beat him up. In terms of the classrooms, Toua remembered that all the Vietnamese, Cambodian, Lao, Thai, and Mong students went to the same class with a Thai teacher. Toua learned later that the program director thought that all the Southeast Asians are Buddhists. That was the commonality that they all had alike so all of them would go to the same class taught by this Thai teacher.

In 1985, Toua enrolled in Nicholas High school. High school was even more challenging than the middle school. At the beginning of each class period, Toua had to rush to find his classes. Sometimes his classes were not even located in the same building. It was different from Laos where the teacher came to the class, or Toua stayed with one teacher for the whole grade. It might take a while before Toua could learn his way around this type of schooling. Toua remembered that the first day of class was very difficult because every classroom looked very similar. He remembered that ·a Mong para-educator (teacher assistant) had to take him by the hand to every class. What a relief! Otherwise, Toua could not have figured out what could have happened to him without the assistance of this Mong para-educator. What a change Toua had to go through in America!

At the college level, Mong students are very disadvantaged. Besides the language barrier and familial responsibility, Mong students lack strategies for studying and the skills of critical thinking and reasoning. They have difficulty passing the English language proficiency tests and coping with the dormitory culture. They lack the research skills to write their papers. Many Mong students are lost in the large university system. Furthermore, some faculty members may not be sensitive to the Mong students' needs.

In 1989, Toua finished high school in Chicago and enrolled at the National College of Lewis. Toua had to leave his family and stayed in a dormitory up north in the suburb of Chicago. No sooner did Toua move in with his roommate than he experienced some difficulties. His roommate played loud music and poker. Toua could not concentrate on his studies at all. Toua preferred to have some time for himself and tried to figure things out by himself. Because of the loud music and poker problem, he attempted to spend more time for his studies at the college library and less time at the dormitory. However, he came back to his room each night, his roommate kept staying up late and continue to play loud music and poker with a group of his friends. Instead of confronting his roommate about this problem, Toua chose the non-confrontational approach to this problem by requesting school officials to transfer him to a different room. The school officials agreed. While one problem was solved, another one emerged. Toua ran into some academic problems relating to his language barrier. His professor assigned some readings and then asked Toua to complete a research project. Toua did not know how to do research. Before he decided to drop out of college, he told a bilingual staff of the program that it was too difficult for him. The bilingual staff told him to "hang in there" and offered additional help to Toua. Toua learned fast and before long he managed to reach his senior year. Later, Toua learned that he had to pass the English competency test. If he did not pass that test, the college would not allow him to graduate from that college. Toua tried to take that test once, then twice, but did not pass the test. Finally, Toua requested his colleagues to tutor him before he attempted the English competency test again for the last time. Toua finally passed the English competency test after three tries.

Then, Toua encountered another problem. He had to do his student teaching in a public school in Chicago. The first day of class was very difficult for Toua. He remembered that he was placed in a middle school in the south side of Chicago where the majority of his students came from diverse backgrounds. His students were much taller than Toua and so he was intimidated by them. When they spoke to Toua, he could hardly understand them the language they used. It seemed like they spoke English dialects that were different from the type of English language that Toua studied in college. Some students communicated with Toua by using slangs and idioms. Some spoke to Toua using African-American English and Chicano English. Each of them seemed to have their own ideolects within the English language.

Besides a heavy teaching schedule, Toua had to set aside additional time to read books in general linguistics, socio-linguistics, English as a Second Language and discourse analysis so that he could understand the various English dialects of his students. This was in order for him to understand the dynamics of his students and to be able to communicate with them effectively if teaching and learning were to take place in his classroom. Through commitment, hard work, and persistence, Toua made it through college and currently teaches in a public school in Milwaukee, Wisconsin since he graduated from college. Toua understood that in order for him to be an effective teacher, he needed to expand his knowledge-base in various disciplines. Toua realized that education was a lifelong process so he continued to enroll in a graduate program at the University of Wisconsin-Milwaukee, Wisconsin. Besides being a husband, a father, a full-time teacher, an elder in the church and a leader in the Mong community, Toua also became a part-time graduate student. In 1998, Toua was awarded a Master's Degree in Education from the University of Wisconsin – Milwaukee.

3. Native Language and Cultural Loss

Mong families have experienced tremendous native language and culture loss. Mong parents and children use both English and Mong to communicate with each other at home. Although Mong understand English to a certain extent, they continue to speak Mong to their children at home since they speak English with a heavy accent which is very embarrassing to them each time they speak English. In the meantime, since Mong children are not proficient in either languages, they continue to speak both English and Mong to their parents and peers. In the opinion of the author, this type of communication is not bilingual, but it is "Monglish" (Mong + English = Monglish). When they communicate with each other, they mix Mong with English and vice versa within one sentence. For example:

[*Koj puas moog tom* school?] meaning [Do you go to school?].
[*Kuv vuv* blanket] meaning [I wear blanket].
[You know *kuv xaav moog* play] meaning [You know I want to play].

Mong children use Mong sentences but mix them with English in this context.

In terms of adjustment, this type of communication has deep educational implications. In a sense, both Mong parents and their children conceptually speak two different languages. The way they see the world and interpret the flow of information semantically operates at two different levels. Mong parents want to preserve their language and culture; whereas their children continue to be educated in English. Therefore, language development occurs for both Mong parents and their children on a continuum at two different levels and at two different rates. In fact, Mong parents and their children do not only speak different languages but they think differently according to the way they were brought up. By the same token, since Mong children were raised in the United States, they have had more exposure to different people, settings, and environment that shaped their views and perspectives in life; whereas their parents have had less opportunity to come into contact with other people from diverse backgrounds. This created a big discrepancy in intergeneration gap and communication between Mong children and their parents, which is the next topic of discussion.

4. Intergenerational Gap

At the elementary school level, Mong parents brought with them the notion of "teachers know best." Their children still come to schools with the concept of respect for teachers. In Laos, their behavior was prescribed and more controlled with little freedom superimposed by dress code, relationship and attitude. Even with the move to America few major problems exist at the elementary level.

Mong female students are under stricter supervision than their male counterparts, and sex segregation is the common social rule. In Laos, many Mong female students must observe strict curfews. For example, it is not customary for Mong girls to be away from home without direct parental and adult supervision. Mong parents have a tendency to overprotect their daughters when dating. Such strict curfews and parental and adult supervision are considered an effective way to maintain cultural ties with the Mong culture. However, some Mong female students start to rebel against their parents, and resent that they are subject to stricter curfews and supervision than their brothers.

At the secondary school and higher education levels, the intergenerational gap between Mong parents and their children seem to widen. At home, Mong students are taught to conform to the Mong social norms of politeness, filial piety, respect and obedience. They are supposed to pay respect to the elderly, to use respectful language, to be submissive at all times, and never to talk back to their parents and the elderly. However, in the United States, they are taught to be assertive, to question and to voice their opinions, whether they agree or disagree. Because intergeneration gap between their Mong children and their parents continues to widen, some children begin to rebel and talk back to their parents and the elderly. This type of behavior is considered atypical and unacceptable in the Mong culture. Since some Mong students think that they have more freedom of choice and that their parents do not know as much as they do, they start to criticize their parents about their knowledge and actions. To the Mong parents, their children's behavior is not acceptable. As a consequence, this creates some skepticism among some Mong parents. They start to question whether the educational approach to teaching and learning in the United States may have been attributed to the cause for their children's misbehavior, disobedience and lack of respect for them. In fact, the real cause could have been something else such as peer pressure and the environment. However, some Mong parents feel that they can no longer tolerate this type of behavior.

Five Mong students were interviewed regarding the interracial dating issue in Chicago. Most of them had between four to twenty American friends throughout each school year. However, their parents did not encourage their friendships with non-Mong. Two Mong students felt that their parents would possibly feel sorry, bad, and unhappy if they dated non-Mong. Their parents preferred them to date someone in their own ethnic group. This is a sample of the multifaceted problems relating to the intergeneration gap between Mong parents and their children.

5. Cultural Differences

Mong children receive different messages from their parents and from their teachers. At one end, they are told to conform to the Mong tradition and customs. At another end, they are told to comply with the social norms of the mainstream society. Since the Mong culture is diametrically different from the many cultures in the United States, Mong children have been caught in the middle between the Mong tradition and those cultures. Let us now return to Toua to illustrate these issues.

Toua's father, Su, is a very traditional man. Su wanted Toua to preserve the Mong tradition. He asked Toua to accompany him to various cities in Illinois, Wisconsin, Minnesota, and California to visit his relatives. Su thought that Toua needed to make connections with his relatives. When Toua graduated from college in 1993, Su approached Toua that it was time for Toua to get married. Toua disagreed with Su stating that he was not ready to assume this responsibility. Su told Toua that Su had a long-time friend, Dan. In order to keep the relationship between Su and Dan's families intact, Su and Dan had arranged for their son and daughter to be married. Toua learned that this pre-arrangement of this marriage ("*qhaib*," meaning "pre-engaged to be married") was made long before Toua was born. Su told Toua that this marriage was to take place as soon as Toua graduated from college.

In Mong culture, it is the parents' responsibility to make sure that their children are all married and have their own families. In this case, Su wanted to make sure that Toua had a wife. When Su asked Dan's daughter's hand for marriage, Toua could not break Su's word. If Toua broke Su's word, Toua would be considered a disobedient and ill-bred child. Toua was taught by many of his teachers and professors that Toua could make his own decision about who to choose as his mate. In a traditional Mong family, when running into such a conflict, Mong children have to give in and obey their parents because the father makes the ultimate and final decision on such a matter. In an interview with a Mong female student who knew the Mong customs very well felt that the Mong tradition, particularly the concept of respect for parents and the elderly should be preserved. Lee stated:

> In Mong customs if you don't respect parents, you are nothing. Customs distinguish a culture. If we don't conserve our customs, we don't conserve our culture. Then, it will disappear.[3]

6. "OverAmericanization"

The Mong now face a new dilemma in education, referred to as "OverAmericanization." This dilemma is the result of an adjustment process where some students combine their own ethnic cultural ego with aspects of the American cultural ego to form a new "hybrid ego." Friedman uses a biological metaphor as she describes a hybrid ego as:

> The result of mixing two separate plants or animals and getting a new type which is often stronger than either of their parents.[4]

Refugee children may likely grow up with such a hybrid identity and have a tendency to become OverAmericanized in language use and norms distinct from the refugees' and Americans.' Their behavior tends to deviate from the norms towards the extreme. Toua witnessed the behavior change of several classmates during his high school years in terms of dressing, language use and hair styles. His friends wore loose, filthy clothing. They dyed their hair in different colors. Many of them wore huge black jackets which Toua felt did not really fit them at all. One of the Voluntary Agency representatives in Chicago described the intergenerational gap between Mong parents and Mong students as continually widening. In an interview, a Voluntary Agency (VOLAG) representative in Chicago asserted that since Mong students had more freedom of choice, some acted "bizarre, troublesome, and hysterical toward their parents."[5]

7. Gang-Related Issues

Jankowski, an expert on gangs, discussed that the reasons a child may join a gang include the opportunity to belong to a group (particularly if a gang provides a strong ethnicity identity) to learn skills, to interact with role models, to achieve a leadership role, to become involved in activity/adventure, and to earn income/secure future.[6] Virtually all studies of gang members, regardless of ethnicity, tend to cite the same issues. Young Mong and other immigrant groups are especially prone to be prey for these gangs as a result of the combination of the other issues cited. During this transitional period, Mong children are particularly at risk. Mong junior high and high school students still struggle in the search for their identity. During the course of investigation with Mong parents, a few parents asserted that their children were the target of gang recruitment. Mong parents have expressed their deepest concerns about the education of their children. They have desperately attempted to seek various mechanisms to keep their children away from gang activities.

In Laos, youth gangs did not exist. When there was an incident of theft or robbery, the individual, if caught, may have been severely punished or killed: "one strike and you are out." The encounter with gang problems in America has emerged into a crisis in Mong education. In 1992, Evenrud conducted a study on "An Educator's Response to Southeast Asian Gangs" in Minnesota and found that Southeast Asian gangs are quite violent.[7]

Toua's experience in this the Mong youth gang provides us an insight on how some Mong parents desperately attempted to deal with their children who involved in gang activities. Toua witnessed the death of a Mong man in Oshkosh, Wisconsin. In 1990, Song (a fictitious name) moved his family of seven people from Chicago to Oshkosh, Wisconsin. According to the story that was told by many Mong eyewitnesses, Song knew that his sixteen-year old son was involved with gangs, but did not know how to deal with this problem. One day, Song decided to put a stop to his son's gang activities. As a consequence, Song had a strong argument with his son. Since his son did not give in to him, Song decided to beat him in the basement of his house. Later, his wife, with his son, reported Song to the police about the incident. As a consequence, Song was arrested for two counts of domestic violence and child abuse. The police and the Wisconsin Child Protective Services (WCPS) testified before a judge against Song and secured a court order to prohibit Song to get close to his wife and children. One day, Song violated this court order and came back to his wife. She called the police. Then, she told him to leave the house because the police were on their way to arrest him. Song left the house, took his gun, and decided to take his own life in his car outside his home in Oshkosh, Wisconsin. His inability to resolve this predicament of his son's involvement in gang activities ultimately leads to Song's suicide.

8. **Role Shift**

Many Mong families experience a shift of traditional roles held by children and parents, father and mother. Since many Mong parents are still illiterate in both English and their own language; whereas their children are literate in English with knowledge and language skills learned in school. A fair number of Mong children end up assuming the role of an interpreter for the family and speak on behalf of the family. Parents, without knowing English, have to stay behind the scene and obtain information through their children or translators. By the same token, in a traditional Mong family, Mong males were the main breadwinners for their families. However, due to lack of English skills, many are incapacitated to assume this role for their families. In reality, in the United States, it is necessary for Mong females to work in order to bring in a second income to meet the family's financial needs and their ends' meet.

In an interview, Koch asserted that Mong females learned English and adjusted faster than their spouses, and shared more responsibilities as providers. Koch witnessed that:

> Mong women are very worn-out. They start to work as soon as they learn some English...and they also continue to be pregnant, deliver babies as well as do other jobs and I think...that is very difficult thing to do.[8]

In the same manner, Mong children learn English rapidly and so they became the translators and spokespersons for their families. Since the fathers do not speak English their role has been limited from a leader to a follower. This role shift has affected many Mong heads of the household.

Toua also noticed that his father, Su, who did not speak English, became very frustrated because he thought that he had lost the respect of his family and of the community. Since he did not speak English, he was at the mercy of his children, particularly Toua. He became the spokesperson for his family. In the meantime, Toua's mother enrolled in English classes. As soon as she spoke English functionally, she took driving lessons and before long she was driving. Su became increasingly frustrated and his role was reduced to "just an old man who did not know what was going on most of the time." The more Su thought about his family, the more he worried about his future. He likened being illiterate to losing his eyesight, where he was totally shut off from the world around him.

9. Misconceptions about the Role of Teachers

Some Mong still have some misconceptions about the roles of parents and teachers. Back in Laos, the Mong entrusted the education of their children into the hands of educators and the school districts. Educators were regarded as their children's "second parents." Mong still believe that teachers are the experts, the people who "know best." This means that educators are responsible to educate "the whole child" including their children's behavior.

Though some educators may argue that they educate the whole child as the Mong claim, but their method and focus are quite different from the perspectives of the Mong parents. Mong parents are extremely concerned about the education of their children. However, they are not vocal in bringing their concerns to schools because they think that teachers already "know best" how to educate their children, believing if they bring their concerns to the teachers, the teachers may consider them offensive.

Mong parents are extremely concerned about morality and the transmission of social values to their children. When their children begin to rebel against them, parents start to question the quality of the education provided to their children. Has the teacher really educated their "whole child" cognitively, socially, mentally, morally and ethically?

10. Lack of Similar Experience

Mong parents lack experience in the American culture that can be passed on to their children. Though all of them have extensive life experiences, the context of their lives is quite different from the cultures of the diverse people in the United States. Their stories seem neither suitable nor appropriate for the new setting. Due to their lack of formal education, Mong parents cannot help their children with school assignments and so Mong children are left to strive for themselves.

Toua remembered an incident that took place when he was still in the middle school. When he could not do his algebra homework, he asked his father to help him. His father stared at him with a sad face for a moment and made no response. Toua felt he could read his father' mind because his father was so frustrated that he did not know what to do. His father said: "I don't even know what algebra is. How can I help you?" Seemingly, Toua had to try to figure out the school assignments by himself. One of Toua's last efforts was to ask his Mong teacher assistant for help. At least, the teacher assistant could explain some algebra concepts to Toua. However, he could only do so much, because he had to travel back and forth among the three campuses in the school district and assisted many Mong students who could not speak English like Toua. His schedules were so full that he could offer very little help.

Current Status of the Mong

Lewis examined *A Profile of the Cambodian, Laotian, and Vietnamese People in the United States* for the National Association for the Advancement of Cambodian, Laotian, and Vietnamese based primarily upon data from the 1990 US Census. This report revealed that the Mong are a very young population. Over 60% are age 17 and under; and 43% have more than 4 children. Almost 72% of the Mong adults have less than a high school education, and over half reported no formal education at all. This lack of formal education in Laos contributed to a low US labor force participation rate of 30%. About 34% of Mong households reported income under $12,000, 31% between $12,000 to $20,000 and 35% above $20,000. These higher figures are often wages for two or three wage-earners per household. About 1.3% of the Mong-Americans aged between 18 and 24 have a bachelor's degree or above, and 3.2% of those age 25 and over.[9] In terms of socio-economics, 63% of the Mong families are still living below the poverty line, so they are unable to provide their children with the basic needs.

Of all the Southeast Asian refugees coming to the United States, the Mong were probably the least technologically sophisticated and the least formally educated. As a result, they face notoriously difficult adjustment problems in almost every aspect of life. The Mong are not only illiterate in their own language but also their lives had been totally disrupted by the long wars in Laos. Since they did not have the skills of reading and writing skills, they were left with very limited marketable skills to make a living in a highly technologically developed nation such as the United States.

The author estimates that close to 100,000 (57%) of the 160,000 Mong currently live in California. This estimate is based on the author's conversations with several Mong leaders throughout the nation. The California Department of Education in 1994 reported that 28,494 Mong students were enrolled in California Public Schools. This report pinpointed that there were only 9 Mong certified teachers in the entire state of California. Therefore, the Mong teacher-student ratio is 1:3,166.[10] Between 1994-1998, there has been some dramatic increase in the number of Mong bilingual teachers who were certified by the California Department of Education from nine (9) to fifty-four (54).

During this period, the number of Mong limited English proficient (LEP) students also increased slightly from 28,494 to 30,551 as of April 1998, and still ranked third behind the Spanish and Vietnamese language groups in California. Therefore, the ratio between Mong certified bilingual teachers to Mong LEP students in California as of April 1998 is 1:566.[11]

According to the statistics compiled by the Energy, Poverty, and Refugee Services (EPRS), State of Wisconsin, Department of Health and Human Services (DHHS), 31,327 Mong currently live in Wisconsin. Based on the statistics provided by the Wisconsin Department of Public Instruction (DPI) as of November 1993, there were 18,254 limited English proficient (LEP) students in Wisconsin. The Mong accounted for 8,785, which is 49% of the total. The Mong are now considered the largest language minority group in Wisconsin.[12] Language continues to a barrier impeding development of their full potential, and impairs their progress toward contributing members in the society. Based upon the author's experience, there were only four Mong certified teachers in Wisconsin during the period 1994-1995, where the Mong bilingual teacher-student ratio was 1:2,197. Newer statistics about the Mong LEP students in Wisconsin are not available.

Education for the Mong is now at the crossroads. As a people, the Mong have always been survivors and have gone through difficult times. Those who made it through to the United States have experienced great turmoil and trauma on their journey, which is not over yet. Many Mong children are now "walking on a very tight rope," and have reached a critical juncture in the road toward personal development. There are many Mong children who have chosen and will continue to choose a positive path - the path of becoming good and contributing citizens. At the same time, there are a few Mong children who have been and are about to choose a negative path fraught with social ills. While not intending to fail, they slowly adopted maladaptive coping strategies. Often no one in their families knows how to guide them towards improvement before and, sadly, for some, it is too late because they have already established a record with the police, or established unhealthy life styles.

Twenty years ago, educators perceived that Mong children brought with them the tradition of respect for parents and teachers. This means that their behavior was prescribed, submissive, and more controlled. Mong children were perceived positively. They were obedient and well-behaved and were classified along with the children of the "model minority myth."

Now, it is estimated that close to 30% of Mong children have somehow been involved with or will involve in gang activities. As more Mong children are born in the United States, the Mong family structure is experiencing a tremendous culture and language loss. As

Mong children begin to lose their cultural ties, they adopt beliefs and behaviors distinct from the Mong tradition. Every day, Mong children have to face the reality of street gangs, prejudice, personal and family problems. They are caught between two cultures, that of their parents and that of their peers.

In addition, nearly an entire generation of the Mong men were trained to be commandos in the special force, "The US Secret Army in Laos" to fight the Communists in Laos. Their skills are not adequately and sufficiently transferable to the American job market. Things that are taken for granted by Americans have to be learned by the Mong. Those Mong who made it to the United States are considered survivors. Though the Mong parents are illiterate, they have great expectations for their children and want their children to become good law abiding citizens and contributing members of society in America. To them, their children are their future social security but while they cannot afford to lose another generation, their skills are not well adapted to deal with their children's problems.

Recommendations

The Mong have special concerns that need special attention. After all, the Mong account for the largest language minority in Wisconsin, perhaps in Minnesota, and are ranked third in terms of the numbers of limited English proficient (LEP) students in California. Therefore, the author would like to encourage educators and leaders in education at the local, state, and federal levels to work with the Mong communities in the United States to respond to their immediate needs. Their social and educational problems clearly point to two areas of greatest needs:

1. Mong youngsters particularly at the upper elementary school, middle high school, and high school levels are the target of gang recruitment. Mechanisms should be put in place to prevent further school dropouts among Mong students;
2. There is an urgent need for Mong professional development nationwide to deal with the growing Mong student population, particularly in the states where there are heavy concentrations of Mong, such as: California, Wisconsin, and Minnesota.

To address the two areas of needs of the Mong students, the author proposes the following recommendations and urges each of the readers to take an active role in opening up the schools for multiple purposes, such as the following:

1. Intervention in Mong Youth Gang Activities
The most pressing problem relates to the Mong children's involvement with gang activities. Local community agencies,

school districts, and state and federal institutions should take a proactive stance to work with Mong parents and communities to find ways to divert Mong children's affiliation with gangs to activities that are positive and constructive. Intervention is urgently needed throughout the major areas impacted with heavy concentrations of the Mong in the United States, such as: Fresno, Merced, Stockton, Sacramento (California), Milwaukee, Green Bay, Oshkosh, Eau Claire, La Crosse, Madison, Wausau (Wisconsin), and St. Paul and Minneapolis (Minnesota).

2. *The Reassertion of Moral Education*

By assessing the overall picture of curriculum in relation to the United States', the author feels that moral education is missing from many school districts' curricula. The author proposes the reassertion of moral education in the curriculum, particularly in the local school districts impacted by the Mong. By examining the structure of a traditional Mong family, we could see that every Mong member was task-specific. They worked hard to contribute to the welfare of the family - the male for bread-winning, the wife for housework, children for tedious and simple manual labor work, and grandparents for baby-sitting and educating the young Mong. The author believes, after carefully re-examining the traditional way of life and the structure of the Mong family, two important aspects of Mong education are missing in the today's curriculum.

First is the lack of Mong grandparents' involvement in the educational process of Mong youngsters. Due to the language barrier, Mong grand-parents withdrew themselves voluntarily from this task of providing informal education to their grandsons and daughters.

Also, today the Mong may have forgotten the importance of the role of their grandparents. In the old days, Mong grandparents used to tell stories to their grandsons and granddaughters night after night. Over a period of time, this story-telling became an effective strategy for imparting core values and morals. Grandparents have applied their teachings for centuries as instructional means to cultivate the mind of the young so Mong youngsters would develop an understanding and pursue excellence, and engage in critical thinking skills, skills within the context of family, community, society, nation-state, and the world.

The reassertion of moral education is intended by this author for Mong youngsters to culminate their knowledge and personal experience to become future productive, contributing and ethical citizens with a conscious mind of familial and social responsibilities. One of the goals is to develop critical reasoning so that they may be able to draw the line between good and evil, between right and wrong.

Secondly, there are tremendous needs for Mong material developments that are culturally sensitive to the needs of the young Mong to develop into well-educated, morally-conscious, and ethical individuals.

3. The Reassertion of Mong Grandparents into the Education Process

Mong grandparents played a very important role in educating the young Mong for centuries. Throughout Mong history, Mong grandparents were left at home for caring, nurturing, cultivating, building strong character, and instilling moral and cultural values in youngsters through story-telling while the rest of the family were busy working in the fields. It was through this oral tradition that young Mong grew up to become upstanding, moral, and ethical individuals and to build strong communities.

When the Mong arrived in the United States, Mong grandparents were forgotten. They were left behind in their own apartments. If we are to be successful in educating the Mong youngsters, it is necessary that we reassert and incorporate the Mong grandparents back into the educational process of the young Mong in various aspects of professional development, material development, and extracurricular activities. Though Mong children have certainly changed from the old days, Mong grandparents can still make a difference in the upbringing of their grandsons and granddaughters.

4. Development of Resources and Educational Programs

School districts with a heavy concentration of Mong families should write proposals to request Title VII funding to provide comprehensive educational services for the Mong children. In Wisconsin, there is only one Title VII funded program in the entire state.

5. Employment of Mong Bilingual and Bicultural Staff

Schools and school districts should be encouraged to employ more Mong bilingual and bicultural staff. This will give both Mong children and parents a sense of a community that they, too, live among a diverse group that will support a climate of high academic expectations.

Leadership and encouragement in the area of Mong staff development and training at all levels are needed. Mong bilingual paraprofessionals (aides, substitute teachers, etc.) could be encouraged to pursue their continuing education with financial support for the extra credits or to work towards certification as bilingual teachers. Developing Mong staff is essential for the implementation of successful programs for educating Mong students and eliminating the illiteracy problems within the Mong communities.

It is essential to recognize that support in providing human services and financial assistance for adequate teacher training of Mong bilingual/bicultural educators be provided to meet the needs of Mong students. The Mong are currently underrepresented in the staff under the **Lau** mandates. Yet, the educational needs of Mong students have not been appropriately met with bilingual teachers who are trained to provide culturally and linguistically responsive instruction. The Mong bilingual teacher-student ratio is 1:2,000 in Wisconsin and 1:3,000 in California in 1995 and 1:566 in 1998.[13] There were only four Mong certified bilingual teachers in the entire state of Wisconsin in 1995 and fifty-four (54) in California in 1998.[14] The author realizes that as of present the numbers of Mong teacher-students may have been narrowed in the past few years. However, due to the shortage of Mong bilingual teachers, the instructional needs for the Mong LEP students in the past have been met largely by ESL teachers and Mong bilingual teacher assistants in various school districts. Some bilingual teacher assistants are recent graduates with bachelor's degrees in various disciplines. Although educational equity has not been adequately addressed, appropriate Mong applicants are currently entering teacher education.

6. *Provision of Bilingual and Bicultural Approach to Learning*
Leadership in school districts and post-secondary educational institutions is needed to provide the bilingual and bicultural education approach to learning. Mong students need to develop academic language as well as social communicative language. Research by Collier and Cummins shows most LEP students need five to seven years of instruction to reach even a moderate level of success in an academic curriculum taught in the second language.[15]

7. *Help from Faculty and Staff*
Encouragement is needed from all faculty and staff to assist the Mong students in making a smooth transition from elementary school level to secondary school level, and from secondary school level to institutions of higher learning.

8. *Opportunity for Professional Development*
School districts should provide all faculty and staff in districts serving Mong students with the opportunity to continue their

professional growth on an ongoing basis to equip them with the knowledge and skills to handle the Mong youth problems.

9. Mong Parental Training

Continued encouragement for the local, state, and federal education agencies to train Mong parents to foster home-school cooperation is critical. Efforts need to be made so parents are able to bring their concerns to schools to improve the education of their children.

10. Development and Implementation of an Inclusive Curriculum

Schools need to be encouraged to develop and implement an inclusive curriculum that is sensitive to the Mong culture. This would bring schools closer to achieving the National Education Goals as well.

Summary

This chapter provided a retrospective comparison of the formal education system in Laos in relation to the U.S.. The discussion includes the multifaceted social and educational problems of Mong students currently faced by the Mong communities and urban American public schools. The chapter presented some of the most challenging contemporary issues that potentially evolve into a crisis in Mong-American education. The author also offers some recommendations for action on how to remedy the situation.

Chapter 6 consists of language development for Mong-speaking students. The chapter includes a brief discussion of the historical development of the Mong orthography, characteristics of Mong-speaking students, a comparative discussion of the similarities and differences for the two major Mong dialects and English in the areas of phonology, morphology, syntax, and semantics. The chapter also probes some of the most typical difficulties for Mong-American students when acquiring English.

Notes

[1] Paoze Thao, "Mong Refugee Resettlement in Chicago (1978-1987): Educational Implications" (Ph.D. Dissertation, Loyola University of Chicago, 1994), pp. 152-201.
[2] Trinity-Arlington Teacher and Parent Training for School Success Project, Model for Use with Limited English Proficient High School Students (Arlington Public Schools, 1986), Home Lesson 2 and 6.
[3] Interview with Pa Chia N. Lee, tape recording, Chicago, Illinois, 16 June 1992 in Paoze Thao, "Mong Resettlement in the Chicago Area (1978-

1987): Educational Implications. Ph.D. Dissertation, Loyola University of Chicago, 1994, pp. 176.

[4] Joan Friedman et al, *Working with Refugees: A Manual for Paraprofessionals*, Vol. III, *Intercultural Counseling and_Interviewing Skills* (Chicago: Travelers Aid/Immigrants Service, 1981), 7.

[5] Interview with Bachnhuyet Le, tape recording, Catholic Charities of Metropolitan Chicago, Chicago, Illinois, 3 June 1992 in Paoze Thao, Mong Resettlement in the Chicago Area (1978-1987): Educational Implications, Ph.D. Dissertation, Loyola University of Chicago, 1994, p. 159.

[6] Martin Sanchez Jankowski, *Islands in the Street: Gangs and American Urban Society* (Berkeley, CA: University of California Press, 1991), pp. 37-62.

[7] Carole J. Evenrud, "An Educator's Response to Southeast Asian Street Gangs," MA Thesis, Hamline University, August 1992.

[8] Interview with Virginia Koch, tape recording, Travelers and Immigrants Aid, Chicago, Illinois, 1 June 1992 in Paoze Thao, Mong Resettlement in the Chicago Area (1978-1987): Educational Implications, Ph.D. Dissertation, Loyola University of Chicago, 1994, pp. 155-156.

[9] James H. Lewis, *A Profile of the Cambodian, Laotian, and Vietnamese People in the United States* (Chicago, Illinois: NAFEA, March 1994).

[10] Language Census Report, California Department of Education, 1994.

[10] Barbara A Bitters and Staff of Equity & Multicultural Education Section, "Pupil Population in Wisconsin Public Schools Protected by Pupil Nondiscrimination Provisions," (Madison, WI: Wisconsin Department of Public Instruction, November 1993).

[11] Language Census Report, California Department of Education, April 1998.

[12] Ibid.; Barbara A. Bitters, 1993.

[13] Language Census Report, California Department of Education, 1994 and April 1998.

[14] Ibid.; Barbara A. Bitters, 1993 and Language Census Report, California Department of Education, 1998.

[15] Anna Uhl Chamot, "Changing Instruction for Language Minority Students to Achieve National Goals," *Proceedings of the Third National Research Symposium on Limited English Proficient Student Issues: Focus on Middle and High School Issues.* Vol. 1. (Washington, DC: US Department of Education, Office of Bilingual Education and Minority Languages Affairs, 1993), p. 55.

Chapter 6

Mong Language Structure and Use: Implications for Mainstream Teachers

Chapter 6 focuses on language development for Mong-speaking students. It consists of a brief discussion on the Mong historical background, the development of the Mong orthography, the characteristics of Mong-American students, a comparative discussion on the two regional Mong dialects and English in the areas of phonology, morphology, syntax, and semantics. This chapter provides a comparison of the various structural aspects of Mong and English language that are essential for language development for Mong-speaking students. This language recognition between similarities and differences in the structure of both languages will not only support but also will guide mainstream teachers in specific areas of language development for Mong-speaking students. The objective of this chapter is to provide linguistic information for classroom teachers and other educators to help accommodate Mong-speaking students for a smooth transition to English-only classrooms.

1. Brief Historical Background

The Mong constitute an ethnic tribe who migrated from China in the eighteenth century to settle in Laos. They assisted France during its colonial rule in Southeast Asia between 1893-1947 and the United States in its Secret War against the Communists in Laos during the Vietnam Conflict between 1962-1975. After the U.S. withdrew its troops from Southeast Asia, the Mong were persecuted for political reasons. In 1976, Congress recognized the Mong as former CIA (Central Intelligence Agency) employees and authorized the U.S. Department of State to admit some Mong refugees to the United States.

As a consequence of the long war in Laos during the Vietnam Conflict (1962-1975), education for Mong adults who are now in the U.S. today had been totally disrupted. Their lack of formal education and marketable skills and their illiteracy in their own language make it difficult for them to live in a highly technologically developed country, such as the United States. Language barriers continue to impede their development to their full potential as contributing members in the society. Based on the statistics provided by the California Department of Education as of March 1, 1996, of the 34,000 Mong students enrolled in California public schools, 31,156 were identified as limited English proficient (LEP) students.[1] This reveals that a crisis in Mong education has emerged.

2. Characteristics of Mong Language

The Mong language was classified by linguistic typologists as a subgroup under the Sino-Tibetan language family of Asia. It is considered one of the pre-Sinitic languages. Arlotto asserted that:

> Within China itself, among the few remaining pre-Sinitic languages we have the Miao-Yao family, spoken by scattered remnants of what once undoubtedly was a widespread and flourishing family.[2]

This means that the Mong had long existed prior to 1300 BC. Chang indicated that the term "Miao" occurred as early as the *Book of Documents* and the Miao people had been in contact with the Chinese at least since the Shang-Chou Dynasty.[3] According to Michael, the Shang Dynasty dated back to 1725-1123 BC and the Chou Dynasty 1123-221 BC.[4]

Despite the Mong language's mutual intelligibility with other languages spoken in Asia, linguists have grouped it with one of the marginalized languages called the Mien under the Mong-Mien (Miao-Yao) language family.[5] Though it is considered a monosyllabic tonal language, it has many disyllabic and polysyllabic words as well. Its lexicons normally consist of a consonant, a vowel, and a tone-marker.

History of the Development of Mong Orthography

There was no historical evidence of any kind before 1909. This suggests that the Mong may not have had a writing system of their own until 1909. Rev. Samuel Pollard, a British missionary of the Bible Mission (formerly the United Methodist Mission) developed "The Pollard Script"[6] that was used to complete the translation of the New Testament into Hwa Miao dialect in China. The bible translation was done under the supervision of Rev. William A. Hudspeth and was published by the British and Foreign Bible Society in 1917.[7] The author reviewed a small specimen of "The Pollard Script," but it is not mutually intelligible to today's Mong in the United States. Except for "The Pollard Script," the Mong still depend upon their oral tradition. They pass on their skills and their social values through old tradition from father to son, from mother to daughter, and from generation to generation.

In the 1950s, with the entry and the emergence of Christianity to Laos, came the development of Mong literacy. Many Mong became Christians through the mission of the Christian and Missionary Alliance (CMA) headquartered in New York (now in Colorado Springs, Colorado). Rev. Xuxu Thao, the first Mong president of the Lao Evangelical Church, recalled and asserted, in his memoirs, that 5,000 Mong and 2,000 Khamu were converted to Christianity in the 1950s.[89] This massive conversion took place when the Andrianoffes, an American missionary couple, were sent to Xieng Khouang province of Laos.

After this massive conversion to Christianity, one of the immediate and critical issues faced by the CMA was the illiteracy of the Mong and Khamu tribes. They both could neither read nor write Lao. Both tribes had no record of having their own writing systems. The following reflected Rev. Xeng Pao Thao's discussion on the origin of the development of Mong literacy.[10] As a consequence, CMA held several conferences in 1951, 1952, and 1953 respectively in Saigon, South Vietnam. The conference resolutions assigned two missionary couples the tasks of developing the orthographies for the Mong and the Khamu tribes. In this manner, Christian literacy and Bible translation could be done in both languages. In turn, they could comprehend the Christian doctrines, which are the foundations of Christian faith.[11]

Barney acknowledged that, in June 1951, he went to Xieng Khouang, Laos to "set the task of reducing the Mong language to writing."[12] Smalley also confirmed this mission with Barney in the same manner in his presentation about the history of the development of the Romanized Popular Alphabet to the Mhong Language Council held at the University of Minnesota on August 12, 1982 in Minneapolis, Minnesota. Smalley asserted that he "went to Luang Prabang province of Laos to study Khamu language and Barney to Xieng Khouang to study Mong Leng."[13] Barney developed proficiency in the Mong language and Romanized it successfully into the Romanized Popular Alphabet (RPA) system. At that time, Barney was referred to as "Thanh Mong" or "Mister Mong." Today, many Mong still remember him as "Thanh Mong." Smalley, trained as a linguist, assisted Barney to refine the RPA.[14] Unfortunately, in 1953, the Communists took over the province of Xieng Khouang, Laos. Though the Mong RPA system was completed and was submitted to the Royal Lao government in 1954 for approval, it was repudiated and was put to a halt. However, the system has been continuously used by the Mong and was officially adopted by the Mong when they arrived in the U.S. in 1976.[15]

The Mong orthography currently and widely used is based on the refinement of the Romanized Popular Alphabet (RPA) system developed by American missionaries of the Christian and Missionary Alliance (CMA), George Linwood Barney and William A. Smalley, in the 1950's. This RPA system has been devised based upon the phonemic principle. Therefore, it is phonemic-based rather than ideographic-based. It depends on the International Phonetic Association (IPA) alphabets. Therefore, this RPA system automatically dichotomizes the Mong into two dialects along the regional pronunciation differences between Mong Leng (Blue Mong) and Hmong Dawb (White Hmong). However, up to the present, there are no writing systems better than the RPA system that can satisfy the Mong's desire. In another words, the RPA system remains the sole writing system that is easy to learn and to use among the Mong, not just in the United States but throughout the world. Even though the RPA system is very consistent and absolutely symmetrical, the writing and spellings vary from dialect to dialect and from ideolect to ideolect (language of the individual) depending on the geographic region from which each of the individual Mong comes.

4. Characteristics of the Mong-speaking Students

Linguistically, the Mong are classified into two major groups: "*Mong Leng*," known as 'Blue Mong' and '*Hmong Dawb*,' known as 'White Hmong.' This classification involves the speakers of the two major regional dialects of the Mong including their new generation of learners enrolled in public schools across the United States and around the world. The following describe their characteristics in greater detail.

Major Dialectal Differences

The Mong are divided into two major regional dialectal groups. One group is referred to Mong Leng (known as "Blue Mong"), and the other as Hmong Dawb (known as "White Hmong"). The fact that there are two distinct Mong linguistic and ethno-cultural groups is supported by Smalley's study.[16] This linguistic division cuts across all the Mong memberships, customs, and various differing Mong who wear costumes of different colors.[17] It is very difficult to estimate the numbers who speak these two regional Mong dialects in the United States. However, many Hmong Dawb (White Hmong) admitted that their ancestors were Mong Leng (Blue Mong). The author speculates that perhaps the two Mong regional dialects are spoken by similar numbers of Mong and perhaps by equal numbers of the population. Though these two Mong dialects seem to be mutually intelligible, there is a difference between them.[18] The difference accounts for about thirty percent (30%) in terms of language and culture between the two Mong groups.

This linguistic difference between the two Mongs can be compared to the pronunciation of British English, American English, and Australian English and vice versa. Some Mong even compare the difference between the two dialects to English and Spanish. Many Mong Leng (Blue Mong) have become bidialectal by switching from one dialect to the other. Practically, Mong Leng (Blue Mong) tend to have an easier time speaking Hmong Dawb (White Hmong) but not the reverse. However, for the most part, the differences tend to center around the pronunciation of certain sound segments and sound combinations that seem to be consistent throughout the two dialects.

In terms of their relationship between Mong Leng (Blue Mong) and Hmong Dawb (White Hmong), the two groups have interwoven their bonds through intermarriage for centuries; however, surprisingly, they have preserved their linguistic and cultural purity, and have respected each other's differences. Both groups have lived with each other harmoniously for centuries. In fact, the two Mongs act to interface with each other for a system of check and balance within the Mong society. The social, religious, educational, and political system of the two groups has its own dynamics that are absolutely symmetrical and well balanced within the Mong society. However, Mong Leng call themselves "Mong" and White Hmong "Hmong."

Language Change

The second major characteristic involves the socio-linguistic aspect of language change. The generation of the Mong-American parents in the United States today have lived through three different countries: Laos, Thailand, and the United States. Some have become 'diglossia,' a term coined by Fergerson.[19] This means that their lexicons have been intermixed with those borrowed from their hosts', e.g. Chinese Mandarin, Lao, French, Thai, and American English. This transmigration from country to country in the last two centuries has resulted in their usage of inter-lingua among themselves. This, in turn, influences their children's language development, e.g.

Blue Mong:	Peb moog tom *tajlaj*, moog yuav *txivlaum fuabxeeb* hab moog saib *cinGna*.
White Hmong:	Peb mus tom tajlaj, mus yuav txivlaum huabxeeb thiab mus saib *cinGna*.
English:	We go to the market, go buy peanuts, and go watch movie
---->	We go to the market, buy peanuts, and watch a movie.

This means that Mong parents have been influenced by Chinese Mandarin, Lao, and French lexicons. In this example, they use Mong sentence patterns but mix with a Lao lexicon, "*tajlaj*, for market," with a Chinese Mandarin lexicon, "*txivlaum fuabxeeb*, for peanuts," and with a French lexicon, "*cinGna*, for movie theater."

Therefore, Mong children enrolled in public schools today have been heavily influenced by their parents' use of language, especially words that were borrowed from Chinese Mandarin, Lao, Thai, French, and American-English. Though they speak English fluently, they could hardly speak proper Mong. In another words, they experience tremendous cultural and language loss. From the examples in Table 13, they basically translate word for word from English to Mong.

Table 13. Mong Children's Use of Language

English	Blue Mong	White Hmong
I wear shoes	Kuv naav qhaus	Kuv hnav qhaus
My father	Kuv tug txiv (my husband) is mixed up with kuv txiv (my father)	Kuv tus txiv (my husband) is mixed up with kuv txiv (my father)

Many Mong students today speak Mong by way of translating directly from English to Mong. The phrase and sentence illustrated above are some of the examples of the way Mong children transfer the concepts of English language (L2) to their native language (L1). What really happens is that Mong students learn the Mong language informally from their parents (L1) without the social and cultural context of the Mong culture. In the meantime, they receive formal education inside and outside of the school setting within the social and cultural context of American culture but without the Mong culture. When they translate the literal meaning from English to Mong without the social and cultural context of the Mong culture, the meanings become semantically anomalous. This direct translation affects the semantics as shown in the example above. This has caused a major concern to Mong parents.

In order to develop bilingual proficiency in Mong and English, many Mong students face a dilemma. They are caught between the macro-culture and the Mong culture, between their native language (L1) and English (L2). Both languages need to be taught and reinforced equally within the social and cultural contexts on the same basis of both cultures. This is a very critical issue in language instruction. Mong students are taught to assimilate to the macro-culture but lack the reinforcement from their parents at home. As a result, they feel disjointed and confused with both cultures and do not know how to respond in a culturally appropriate manner. This is the reason why language instruction cannot take place without the social and cultural contexts. In another words, language instruction cannot occur in isolation but needs to be totally immersed naturally by integrating with the content areas in both Mong and English. Mong students have been taught formally at schools in academic settings without any reinforcement from the social and cultural context from their parents at home. They also learn the Mong language informally at home without any academic support for the Mong language from school. Thus, the gap between home and school continues to widen. As a consequence, language use for Mong children becomes disorderly and confused.

5. A Comparative Discussion on the Two Mong Regional Dialects

The linguistic difference between the Blue Mong and the White Hmong may be compared to British English and Australian English and vice versa. Several Mong compared them to English and Spanish. Though many Mong Leng (Blue Mong) have become bidialectal by switching from one dialect to another, this does not mean that they are fluent speakers of White Hmong. Practically, Mong Leng tend to have an easier time speaking White Hmong dialect but most likely not the reverse. For the most part, Purnell and Smalley indicated that the differences between these two regional dialects center around the pronunciation of certain sound segments and sound combinations that seem to be consistent throughout the two dialects.[20]

In the past, some authors have used the term, "*Mong Leng*" as synonymous with the term "Blue Mong." Another term seems to be widely used by 'White Hmong' to refer to "*Mong Leng*" as "*Mong Ntsuab*" (Green Mong). The author prefers the term "Mong Leng" since "Mong Ntsuab" has a negative connotation attached to it that every Mong Leng objects to when the term is used. They find it offensive and is intimidating by its use. The term "*Mong Ntsuab*" (Green Mong) refers to a subgroup of the Mong who anachronistically practiced a cult of cannibalism. The author believes that this subgroup of the Mong is no longer in existence. Though the two Mong dialects are considered mutually intelligible in certain contexts, Smalley asserted that their lexicons "seem to be completely different"[21] and "do not seem to correspond with each other at all."[22] The following table illustrates some of the words that are different in the two regional Mong dialects.

Table 14. Lexical Differences of the Two Mong Regional Dialects

Blue Mong	White Hmong	Meaning in English
Dlaim choj	daim pam	a blanket
Ntsab	Txhuv	rice
Paamdlev	Puamhub	mint
Txivkwj	Yawglaus	husband of aunt (uncle)
Pujnyaaj	Phauj	aunt
Lub qwg	Lub laujkaub-fwj	a kettle
Taujqab	Taujdub	lemon grass
Lub xaabcum	Lub kos	Fire iron
Tug kaabcuam	Tus khib	An instrument used to carry firewood on the back

Several researchers also noted that the difference in the majority of the Mong lexicons lies in the pronunciation with the exception of the suppletive forms. This pronunciation difference between *Mong Leng* (Blue Mong) and *Hmong Dawb* (White Hmong) is fairly consistent throughout the sounds, sound segments and/or sound combinations. They can be predictably matched by their counterpart corresponding sounds between Mong Leng (Blue Mong) and Hmong Dawb (White Hmong).[23] Table 15 illustrates a systematic sound correspondence between the two Mong regional dialects.

Table 15. Sound Correspondence Between the Two Mong Dialects

Corresponding Sounds	English Meaning	Blue Mong	White Hmong
Consonants	Mong/ Hmong	/m/ Moob	/hm/ Hmoob
	heavy	/ny/ nyaav	/hny/ hnyav
	a bag	/n/ naab	/hn/ hnab
	water	/dl/ dlej	/d/ dej
	to run	/dlh/ dlha	/dh/ dhia
	to break	/ndl/ ndlais	/nt/ ntais
	the sound of boiling rice porridge	/ndlh/ ndlhijndlhuj	/nth/ nthijnthuj
Irregular consonant	to respect	/f/ fwm	/h/ hwm
Vowels	a foreigner	/aa/ maab	/a/ mab
	a woman's dress	/a/ taabtab	/ia/ tabtiab
Irregular vowel sounds	to say	/a/ has	/ai/ hais
	a female	/u/ puj	/o/ poj (pog)
	to cause	/ua/ kuas	/o/ kom
	to go	/oo/ moog	/u/ mus
Tone	a horse	/--g/ neeg	/--s/ nees

Therefore, the dialectal difference between the two Mong regional dialects and language change have been the two major characteristics that have impacted Mong-speaking children's acquisition of dual language on a daily basis. The rationale for this impact is caused by the unequal and unbalanced reinforcement of both English and Mong languages from both cultures.

Besides this linguistic difference, another way to classify the Mong into various subgroups is by way of the colors of their costumes and tradition. The Mong can be classified as *Mong Sib*, *Mong Dlub* (Black Mong), *Mong Ntsuab* (Green Mong*), *Mong Txhaij* (Striped Mong), *Mong Quasnpaab* (Flowery Mong), *Hmong Dawb* (White Hmong).[24] Quincy pointed out that this classification took place during the Shang Dynasty (1600 - 800 BC). Following Tseu You's (a Mong leader) defeat, Hang Ti (or the Yellow Emperor) reorganized the Mong into the eight-family system, implemented a policy of forced migration to the eight settlements, and coerced them to abandon their traditional lifestyle from semi-nomadic farmers to sedentary peasants.[25] However, this was not a linguistic classification.

Mong Leng (Blue Mong) are proud of their true name which translates to **"Veins of the Mong**," implying that they carry the life blood for all Mong. White Hmong refers to the color of their ceremonial dress, and there is no negative connotation attached to it. Throughout the centuries, the two regional Mong dialects could be mutually intelligible by the members of the two groups. The two Mong groups have interwoven their bonds through intermarriage for centuries; however, surprisingly, they have preserved their linguistic and cultural purity, and have respected each other's differences. Both have lived with each other harmoniously for centuries. In fact, the two Mong act to interface with each other for a system of check and balance, but within the Mong community. The social, religious, educational, and political system has its own dynamics, that are absolutely symmetrical and very well-balanced within the Mong society. However, the Blue Mong (Mong Leng) called themselves "Mong" and White Hmong (Hmong Dawb) "Hmong."

6. Mong Language Structure vs. English

The following paragraphs describe the characteristics of the Mong language compared with English in the areas of phonology, morphology, and syntax. The areas of difficulties for Mong-speaking students in learning American English will also be presented.

Mong Phonology

The Mong language shares the same sentence structure with American English. A Mong sentence structure depicts a **Subject +**

Verb + Object (SVO) pattern like American English, e.g. *Kuv hlub koj*. "*Kuv* (subject) + *hlub* (Verb) + *koj* (Object)" that transliterates into "I love you" in English. Notice that each word ends with a consonant. These endings are not consonantal phonemes as in American English but they represent the tone markers, e.g. Ku<u>v</u> (mid rising tone), hlu<u>b</u> (high tone) ko<u>j</u> (high falling tone) in this context. These endings are tone-markers and the Mong do not pronounce them like the inflectional endings as in American English. Please keep in mind that the Mong language is non-derivational. In other words, derivational morphology in Mong does not exist. The Mong maintains the same form of the words so derivational morphology is not an essential part of the Mong language.

Phonologically, Mong is a tonal language. Though linguists have classified it under the monosyllabic language family, despite its monosyllabism, the Mong language also contains a sizable number of disyllabic and polysyllabic words as well. A typical Mong lexicon consists of a consonant plus a vowel and a tone marker, e.g. "Kuv" **K** is a consonant, **u** - the vowel, and **v** - the tone-marker. General speaking, the Mong language is comprised of sixteen (16) vowel phonemes, sixty-three (63) segmental phonemes, and eight (8) different tone markers. The following paragraphs will provide a discussion of each in detail.

1) *Mong Vowel Phonemes*

Mong language consists of sixteen (16) vowel phonemes: ten (10) monophthongs [six (6) oral vowels, and three (3) nasal vowels - see Table 16] and six diphthongs (a combination of two single vowels[26] or a single vowel plus a glide).[27]

a)   Ten (10) monophthongs: six (6) oral monophthongs and
     three (3) nasal monophthongs:

- Six oral monophthongs: /i/, /e/, /w/, /u/, /o/, /a/, /ə/
- Three (3) nasal monophthongs: /ee/[eŋ], /aa/ [aŋ]*
  and /oo/ [oŋ]

b)   Six (6) diphthongs:

- Three (3) open diphthongs: /ia/**   /ua/   /uə/
- Three (3) close diphthongs: /ai/,   /aw/   /au/

Note: * used by Blue Mong only
        ** used by Whte Hmong only

Table 16. Mong Vowel Phonemes

	Front		Central		Back	
	Un-round-ed	Round-ed	Un-round-ed	Round-ed	Un-round-ed	Round-ed
High	/i/	/w/				/u/
Middle (Nasal)	/e/ /ee/ [eŋ]		/ə/			/o/ /oo/ [oŋ]
Low (Nasal)					/a/ /aa/ [aŋ]	

2) Mong Consonantal Phonemes

There are sixty-three (63) segmental phonemes used by both Mong regional dialects: Nineteen (19) single consonants, twenty-four (24) double consonantal blends, sixteen (16) triple consonantal blends, and four (4) quadruple consonantal blends. Table 17 illustrates the existing phonemes in Mong with some exceptions.

a)   Nineteen (19) single consonants

```
p    t    d**   r    c    k    q    ?    f
x    s    h     v    z    m    n    l    w
y
```

b)   Twenty-four (24) double consonantal blends

```
pl   dl**  d    ts   tx   ph   th   rh   ch
kh   qh    np   nt   nr   nc   nk   nq   xy
ml   ny    ng   hl   hm** hn** ng
```

c)   Sixteen (16) triple consonantal blends

```
plh  dlh*  tsh  txh  nph  npl  nth  ndl  nts
nrh  nch   ntx  nkh  nqh  hml**     hn**
```

d)   Four (4) quadruple consonantal blends:

```
nplh  ndlh  ntsh  ntxh
```

Table 17. Mong Consonant Phonemes

Manners of Articulation		Labial		Apico-Dental		Apico-Alvelor			Palatal		Velar		Glottal
		bi-labial	labio-lateral release	labio-dental	apico dental	apico alvelar lateral	apico alvelar affricate	apico post alveolar	palatal	palatal affricate release	velar	back velar	glottal
Stops and Affricates	vl.* un-aspirated	p	pl		t	(d)	ts		c	tx	k	q	?
	vl. aspirated	ph	plh		th	dlh**	tsh	rh	ch	txh	kh	qh	
	vd.unaspirated					dl**		r					
	vd.* prenasal unaspirated	np	npl		nt	ndl**	nts		nc	ntx	nk	nq	
	vd. prenasal aspirated	nph	nplh		nth	ndlh**	ntsh		nch	ntxh	nkh	nqh	
Fricatives	vl.			f			x		s	xy			h
	vd.			v					z				
nasal	vl.	(hm)	(hml)		(hn)					(hny)			
	vd.	m	ml		n					ny	ng* [ŋ]		
Liquid	vl.				hl								
	vd.				l								
Glides				w***									

Adapted and compiled by the author.

Source: William A. Smalley, The Problems of Consonants and Tone: Hmong (Meo, Miao)," *Phonemes and Orthography: Language Planning in Ten Minority Languages of Thailand* (Pacific Linguistics Series C. No. 43), ed. By William A. Smalley, 85-123) (Canberra: Australian National University, 1976), 89.

And Martha Suzan Ratliff, "The Morphological Functions of Tone in White Hmong," Ph.D. Dissertation, University of Chicago, 1986), 16.

Remarks: * vl. stands for voiceless and vd. for voiced.

** Mong Literacy Volunteer, Inc., "Phoneme Spelling Change," Minutes of Meeting on 13 September 1980 from tl, tlh, ntl, ntlh, and [n] to dl, dlh, ndl, ndlh, and ng (Joliet, IL: Mong Literacy Volunteer, Inc, 1980).

*** Phoneme addition proposed by Rev. Xeng PaoThao in consultation with George Linwood Barney. Original () are phonemes used only with White Hmong (Hmoob Dawb).

3) Eight (8) Mong Tone Markers

In addition, the Mong lexicons could not have been fully constructed without the tone-markers. A lexicon in the Mong language always consists of a consonant, a vowel, and a tone-maker. The tone-marker is always situated at the end of each word or always follows each vowel. The following letters represent the Romanized Popular Alphabet (RPA) symbols for the tone-markers for the Mong language. There are eight (8) different vocal tones. (See Table 18 for the Mong Tone Makers

Table 18. Mong Tone Markers

RPA Symbol	Blue Mong	White Hmong	Meaning
-b high	cua**b**	cua**b**	trap
	ti**b**	ti**b**	to pile up
-j high falling	cua**j**	cua**j**	number nine
	ti**j**	ti**j**	older siblings
-v mid-rising	cua**v**	cua**v**	counterfeit
	ti**v**	ti**v**	to resist, to oppose, to opt against
-mid	cua-	cua-	wind
	ti-	ti-	near
-s mid low	cua**s**	cua**s**	father of son's wife
	ti**s**	ti**s**	wing, to name
-g mid low breathy	cua**g**	cua**g**	to reach to
	ti**g**	ti**g**	to turn to
			to reverse
			to spin around
-m low glottalized	cua**m**	cua**m**	to press together
	ti**m**	ti**m**	because of
-d predictable variant of /-m/	-	-	-
	ti**d**	ti**d**	there, over there

4) No Stress in Mong as in English

One of the characteristics that distinguishes American English from Mong is the use of stress and intonation. In English, one or more syllables in each content word is stressed, e.g.

a) subject   (noun)
   The subject of a story ...(The stress falls on the first syllable)
   subject   (verb)
   He'll subject us to his boring stories (the subject falls on the
   second syllable)

b) pervert   (noun)
   My neighbor is a pervert (the stress falls on the first syllable)
   pervert   (verb)
   Don't pervert the idea (the stress falls on the second syllable)

5) No Intonation in Mong as in English

One of the characteristics that distinguishes English from Mong is the use of intonation. Mong language uses the eight different tones to distinguish the semantics of the words (see the discussion of Mong tones discussed previously in this chapter). Whereas in English, pitch plays an essential role in the lexicons and semantics (or the meanings) of the sentences, e.g.

a. What did you put in my | drink, | Tom?

b. What did you put in my drink, Tom?

In sentence a) the questioner asks what Tom put in the drink; whereas the questioner in sentence b) is asking if someone put Tom in the drink.

Mong Morphology

Morphology is defined as "the study of the internal structure of words; the component of the grammar which includes the rules of word formation."[28] As previously discussed, Mong is a non-inflection language. Most of the lexicons consist of monosyllables, sometimes disyllables and polysyllables. However, they do not change their forms. Since it does not take on the affixes (prefixes and suffixes) as in English, English morphology is difficult for Mong-speaking students. The following illustrate some of the difficulties that Mong-speaking students may encounter:

1) No -s/es inflections as in English

The Mong language maintains the same form. It does not carry -s/es inflections as in plural forms as well as in third person singular present tense forms as in English, such as:

Blue Mong: <u>Kuv   muaj ib tug*   cwjmem</u> (singular)
White Hmong:<u>Kuv   muaj ib tus** cwjmem</u> (singular)
English: I   have a (clf)*** pen.

Blue Mong: <u>Kuv   muaj ntau   tug cwjmem</u> (plural)
White Hmong:<u>Kuv   muaj ntau   tus cwjmem</u> (plural)
English: I have many (clf.) pen<u>s</u>.

Both Mong: <u>Kuv   yuav ib lub   tsho</u> (singular)
English: I buy a (clf.) shirt.

Both Mong: <u>Kuv   yuav ntau lub   tsho</u> (plural)
English: I buy many (clf.) shirt<u>s</u>.

Blue Mong: <u>Nwg   yuav kaum lub tsho</u> (plural)
White Hmong:<u>Nws   yuav kaum lub tsho</u> (plural)
English: He/she buy<u>s</u>   ten (clf.) shirt<u>s</u>.

Note: *   Blue Mong use mid low breathy tone /-g/
      **   White Hmong use mid low tone /-s/
    (clf.) is an abbreviation of a classifier

2) Adding the word "kev" to Mong lexicons to form nouns in Mong

In Mong, when adding the work "<u>**kev**</u>" in front of a word, it changes all the grammatical lexical categories to nouns or becomes nouns. Though inflectional morphology does not exist in Mong, derivational morphology does exist. In English, when we add prefixes (pre-, circum-, trans-, post-, etc.) and suffixes (-ment, -ion, -ance, -ion or -ia, -ty, -ism, etc.) to a root stem, the new derived word will normally change the grammatical category. By the same token, inflectional morphemes also co-exist with derivational morphemes and tend to surround the derivational morphemes, e.g. neighborhood --> neighborhood<u>s</u> or I sing/he sing<u>s</u>. However, in Mong, there are no noun declensions as in English (See Table 19 - Derivational Morphology in Mong and in English).

Table 19. Derivational Morphology in Mong and English

<u>Blue Mong</u>	<u>White Hmong</u>	<u>English Meaning</u>
<u>Kev</u> tswjfwm	<u>**kev**</u> tswjfwm	govern**ment**
<u>Kev</u> qeeglug	<u>**kev**</u> qeesleeg	criter**ion** (criter**ia**)

Kev txavtawm	kev txiavtawm	subtract**ion**
Kev thuam	kev thuam	critic**ism**
Kev paabcuam	kev pabcuam	assist**ance**
Kev puamtsuaj	kev puamtsuaj	casual**ty**

3) No Grammatical Gender in Mong as in French, Spanish, or English

In Mong, there are no grammatical genders (like masculine or feminine) as in French, Spanish, or English e.g. **le** jardin (the garden), **la** maison (the house). Though the Mong uses " tub," meaning "son" and " ntxhais," meaning "daughter" to denote gender (masculine or feminine), the Mong language does not have grammatical gender like American English, e.g.

Blue Mong: *txaistog* (for both masculine and feminine)
White Hmong: *txaistos* (for both masculine and feminine)
English: wait**er** (masculine)   wait**ress** (feminine)

Blue Mong: **tub** *fuabtais* (masculine)
                ntxhais *fuabtais* (feminine)
White Hmong: **tub** *huabtais* (masculine)
                ntxhais *huabtais* (feminine)
English: prince (masculine)   princess (feminine)

The difference between American English and Mong is in the use of the term "**tub**" [meaning 'son'] or "**ntxhais**' [meaning 'daughter'] placing in front of " **fuabtais**" or " **huabtais**" [meaning 'king']. This compound noun marks the gender of the lexicon. In addition, since the Mong lived through China, Laos, the refugee camps in Thailand, and the U.S., they have borrowed words from ancient Chinese Mandarin, Lao, French, Thai, and American English lexicons as illustrated in Table 20, Table 21, and Table 22.

4) Words Borrowed from Ancient Chinese Mandarin

It is estimated that the Mong borrowed approximately ten (10 %) percent of their lexicons from ancient Chinese Mandarin. For example, all the words that end with '**-xeeb**' were borrowed from ancient Chinese Mandarin.

Table 20. Words Borrowed from Ancient Chinese Mandarin

Blue Mong	White Hmong	English meaning
Txivlaum fuabxeeb	txivlaum huabxeeb	peanut
Tshwjxeeb	tshwjxeeb	special
Thaajyeeb	thajyeeb	peaceful
Pheejyig	pheejyig	reasonable, cheap

5) *Words Borrowed from Lao*

Table 21. Words Borrowed from Lao

Blue Mong	White Hmong	English meaning
Khoom	khoom	things
Xabnpum	xabnpum	soap
Tajlaj	Tajlaj	market
Faisfab	faisfab	electricity
laa-voos	la-voos	dancing

6) *Words Borrowed from French*

Table 22. Words Borrowed from French

Blue Mong	White Hmong	French	English meaning
Kilomev	kilomev	Kilomätre	kilometer
Faabkis	Fabkis	Franáais	French
Cine (ma)	Cine (ma)	Cinma	Cinema or movie

7) *Words Borrowed from English*

Table 23. Words Borrowed from American English

Blue Mong)	White Hmong	English meaning
Amelikas	Amesliskas	America
Okay	okay	okay
tshawj	tshawj	church

Mong Syntax

1) Word Order

Syntactically, Mong sentences follow the English sentence patterns of SVO (Subject, Verb, and Object), e.g.

Both Mong: <u>Kuv   hlub   koj</u>.
English: I   love   you.

However, the lexical category of adjective in Mong does not follow the word order of the English pattern. In English, adjectives normally precede nouns, e.g. a <u>big</u> house. Whereas in Mong, the adjectives are placed after the nouns similar to French, e.g. <u>lub tsev luj</u> ("the house big" instead of "the big house" as in English). Therefore, word order may be difficult for Mong speaking students.

2) Inflection Endings

a)   In Mong, there are no -ed forms in past tenses as in English,

Both Mong: <u>Kuv   hlub   koj   nubnua</u> (present)
English: I   love   you   today.

Both Mong: <u>Kuv   hlub   koj   tsebnua</u> (past tense)
English: I   lov<u>ed</u> you   last year.

Though Mong language does not take on any inflections in the past tense forms as in American English, this does not mean that the Mong do not have tenses. They express their tenses through adverbial phrases, such as today, yesterday, tomorrow, etc.

b) Nǫ -ing Forms in Participles in Mong

There are no -ing forms in participles in Mong as in American English,

Both Mong: <u>hlub</u>   --> <u>hlub</u>
English: love   --> lov<u>ed</u> --> lov<u>ing</u>

3) Constructing Interrogative Sentences in Mong

Mong do not move subject and verb around in interrogative sentences as in English, but insert the word **"puas"** (question) between the subject and the verb or in front of the verb to turn the affirmative sentence into an interrogative sentence, e.g.

Both Mong:	Kuv	**puas**	hlub	koj?
English:	I	(question)	love	you?
------>	Do	I	love	you?

Both Mong:	Koj	**puas**	hlub	kuv?
English:	You	(question)	love	me?
____>	Do you		love	me?

4) Constructing Negative Sentences in Mong

For negative sentences, Mong insert the word **"tsi"** (not) before the verb or the modal auxiliaries, such as:

Both Mong:	Kuv	**tsi**	hlub	koj.
English:	I	(negative for not)	love	you.
----->	I	do not	love	you.

Both Mong:	Kuv	**tsi**	noj	mov.
English:	I	(negative for not)	eat	rice.
----->	I	do not	eat	rice.

5)   No Verb Conjugation

In Mong, there are no verb conjugations as in French or English. Conjugation is an act or a presentation of a complete set of inflected forms of verbs while being conjugated to signify the different tenses and mood as illustrated in the examples of French and English sentences as compared to those of the Mong below:

Blue Mong:	Kuv	hu	ib	zaaj*	nkauj(present)
White Hmong:	Kuv	hu	ib	zaj**	nkauj.
French:	Je	chante	une(clf.)***	chanson.	
English:	I	sing	a (clf.)***	song.	

Blue Mong:	Kuv	hu ib	zaaj*	nkauj (past tense)
White Hmong:	Kuv	hu ib	zaj**	nkauj.
French:	J'ai	chanté une(clf.)***chanson.		

English: I   *sang* a (clf.)***song.

Blue Mong: <u>Kuv   hu ib zaaj*</u>   <u>nkauj</u> (future)
White Hmong: <u>Kuv   hu ib zaj**</u>   <u>nkauj</u>.
French: Je chant*erai* une (clf.)***   chanson.
English: I   *will sing* a (clf.)***   song.

Note: *   "zaaj" is a classifier used in front of nouns like 'nkauj'
               in Blue Mong.
       ** "zaj"   is a classifier used by White Hmong (see more
               discussion in the typical Mong classifiers.
       *** (clf.) stands for classifier and is used in front of
               certain Mong nouns

- ## Mong Classifiers

The Mong language is different from American English in its use of classifiers. The Mong always use classifiers (clf.) in front of nouns to denote or express morphology or suffix. The Center for Applied Linguistics defines the function of classifiers as:

Word which comes just before the noun, and which combine with it and its modifiers in several ways to express many of the ideas that English expresses by means of suffixes -- like plurals, possessives, and so on, e.g. a glass of water, a stick of gum.[29]

Both Mong: <u>ib lub   tsev</u>
English: a (one) (clf.)   house

Blue Mong: <u>ib dlaim   tab</u>
White Hmong: <u>ib daim   tiab</u>
English: a (one) (clf.)   dress

Table 24 consists of a list of the Mong classifiers that must be used in front of the different types of nouns to denote or express morphology.

Table 24. Typical Mong Classifiers

Blue Mong	White Hmong	Use with
Tsaab	tsab	paper, inanimate things
Tug	tus	people or animals
Zaaj	zaj	a paragraph, a verse
Tsob	tsob	trees or plants
Lub	lub	inanimate objects

Dlaim	daim	paper
Raab	rab	knife, hammer
Pawg	pawg	a pile of inanimate things
Paab	pab	group of people and animals
Haiv	haiv	ethnic groups
Thooj	thooj	inanimate things (bundle)
Raaj	raj	something long in shape
Phau	phau	book
Phaab	phab	a page
Nthwv	nthwv	smoke, wind, steam
Txuj	txoj	something round and long
Txhais	txhais	a pair, arms and legs
Chaav	chav	shape in square
Teg	tes	something with a handful
Pob	pob	something with a bundle

7) Typical Difficulties for Mong-Speaking Students

The following represent some of the most typical difficulties that Mong students may have and may encounter in the classrooms:

1) *Pronunciation Problems*

Mong students may have difficulties pronouncing the following sounds in English:

Beginning Sounds:

/b/	as in bat	/v/ as in vat	/w/ as in win
/z/	as in zone	/j/ as in suggest	/z/ as in vision
/θ/	as in thick	/t/ as in tick	/ð/ as in they
/d/	as in day		

These pronunciation problems are the result of the direct transference from Mong consonantal sounds that may or may not correspond directly with English mainly due to the places and the manners of articulation (See Table 25 for more details).

Table 25. Sound Articulation Correspondence between Mong vs. English

English Sounds	Mong Sound s	English place of articulation	Mong Place of Articulatio n	English Manner of Articulation	Mong Manner of Articulation
/p/ as in spin	/p/	bilabial	bilabial	voiceless stop unaspirated	voiceless unaspirated stop & affricate
/p/	/ph/	bilabial	bilabial	voiceless stop aspirated	voiceless aspirated stop & affricate
/b/	/np/	bilabial	bilabial	voiced bilabial	voiced pre-nasalized unaspirated & affricate
/t/ as in stick	/t/	alveolar	apico-dental	voiceless stop with no aspiration	voiceless unaspirated stop & affricate
/t/ as in tick	/th/	alveolar	apico-dental	voiceless stop with aspiration	voiceless aspirated stop & affricate
/d/ as in dog	/dl/	alveolar	apico-alveolar lateral	voiced stop	voiced unaspirated stop & affricate
/d/ as in dog	/d/	alveolar	apico-alveolar lateral	voiced stop	voiced unaspirated stop & affricate
/k/ as in skin	/k/	velar	velar	voiceless unaspirated stop	voiceless unaspirated stop & affricate
/k/	/kh/	velar	velar	voiceless aspirated stop	voiceless aspirated stop & affricate
/g/	/nk/	velar	velar	voiced stop	voiced pre-nasalized unaspirated stop & affricate
/l/	/l/	alveolar	apico-dental	voiced lateral liquid	voiced lateral liquid
-	/hl/	-	apico-dental	-	voiceless lateral liquid
/r/	/r/	alveolar	apico-post-alveolar	voiced liquid	voiced unaspirated stop & affricate
-	/rh/	-	apico-post-alveolar	-	voiceless aspirated sop & affricate
/w/	/w/	bilabial and/or velar	labio-dental	glide	glide
/z/	/z/	alveolar	palatal	voiced	voiced fricative

				fricative	
/j/ or /dz/	/nts/	palatal	apico-alveolar-affricate	voiced affricate	voiced pre-nasalized unaspirated stop & affricate
-	/hm/	-	bilabial	-	voiceless nasal aspirated
-	/ml/	-	labio-lateral release	-	voiced nasal
-	/hml/	-	labio-lateral release	-	voiceless nasal aspirated
/n/	/n/	alveolar	apico-dental	nasal	voiced nasal
-	/hn/	-	apico-dental	-	voiceless nasal
-	/ny/	-	palatal-affricate release	-	voiced nasal
-	/hny/	-	palatal-affricate release		
/ng/ [ŋ] as in sing	/ng/ [ŋ]	velar (only occur syllable initially	velar (occur both syllable initially and finally	velar	nasal
/θ/	-	interdental	-	voiceless fricative	-
/ð/	-	interdental	-	voiced fricative	-

5) *All Consonant Clusters Pronounced as Digraphs in English*

Mong consonantal blends are pronounced as digraphs in English. Therefore, Mong children may have difficulties with the spelling of many English silent consonantal clusters, e.g.:
corps/s/   thr/θr/ough   bath/θ/ bathe/ð/

b) *All Ending Sounds Are Not Pronounced in Mong*

Mong speakers do not pronounced all the ending sounds of consonants or vowels at all like American-English, e.g. ba/t/, bat/s/, including those allomorphs, which are the phonetic variants of the regular plural morphemes and of the past tense morphemes (see example below). Therefore, it is difficult for Mong-speaking students to pronounce these plural and past tense allomorphs as in /-s/, /-z/, /-ðz/ and /-d/, /-t/, and /-ðd/:
Plural allomorphs: /-s/   /-z/   /-ðz/

cat<u>s</u> /s/   dog<u>s</u> /z/   bush<u>es</u> /-∂z/
Past tense allomorphs: /-d/   /-t/   /-∂d/
called /-d/   walked /-t/   wanted /-∂d/

c) *Vowel Sounds*

Besides the three nasal vowel phonemes (/ee/, /aa/, and /oo/), the Mong language consists of six vowel phonemes: /i/, /e/, /w/, /u/, /o/, and /a/ as opposed to the twelve English vowel phonemes. This means that the Mong do not have the following lax (short) vowel phonemes corresponding to the English vowel phonemes as following:

/I/ as in   bit   /ɛ/ as in   bet
/U/ as in   butt   /æ/ as in   bat

The difficulties lie within their confusion in distinguishing the three new lax (short) vowel phonemes (/I/, /ɛ/, /U/ in English and the tense vowel /ĕ / phonemes with the tense (long) vowel phonemes in Mong. These vowel phonemes are not compatible in Mong. In other words, the Mong do not have these vowel phonemes in their repertoire.

bet/ɛ/   vs.   bait/e/   vs. bat /æ/
bit /I/   vs.   beat/I/

d) *Vowel Digraphs*

Mong children may have problems with the English vowel digraphs. Vowel digraphs are the combinations of two vowel sounds illustrated by Fromkin and Rodman[30] as following:

oo   wo   ough   ew   ue   oe
as in: t<u>oo</u>   t<u>wo</u>   thr<u>ough</u>   thr<u>ew</u>   cl<u>ue</u>   sh<u>oe</u>

The spelling of these vowel digraphs in American-English may cause some confusion to Mong-Speaking students. This is because of their unfamiliarity with the forms of the English vowel digraphs. All the digraphs presented in the examples above are pronounced with the /u/ sound. However, /oo/ is a nasal vowel phoneme in Mong and is pronounced /oŋ/ instead of /u/.

130   *Mong Language Structure and Use*

e) *Modal Auxiliaries*

The role of modals, or auxiliaries, modal auxiliaries, or helping verbs in the semantics of American-English can be expressed for the degree of greater consideration, politeness, tentativeness, permission, ability, possibility, willingness, obligation, prediction, and so on. To a certain extent, modal auxiliaries in American English should be taught to Mong-Speaking students so that they can know the importance of language use in English. Otherwise, when they use the English language, it seems to be harsh and rude. Those students who know how to use modal auxiliaries will know how to express themselves in an appropriate manner. Those who use English without knowing the proper use of appropriate modal auxiliaries will make language rude and impolite for the tone is very demanding (see more details in Thao's study) compared with the corresponding modal auxiliaries in Mong versus English.[31] Their semantics are synonymous with American English modals (See Table 26).

Table 26. Mong and English Modals

Blue Mong Modals	White Hmong Modals	English Modals
Tau	Tau	can, could, may, might
Yuav	Yuav	will, would, shall
Yuavtsum	Yuavtsum	must, would, should
Yeejyuav	Yeejyuav	need
Ibtxwm	Ibtxwm	used to
Muaj peevxwm	Muaj peevxwm	dare, have the ability to
Maamle, le-maam, mam, le	Mamli, li-mam, mam, li	may, might, shall, should

Mong Verb Formation

a) Mong Verbs Taking the Same Forms

Mong verbs take the same forms when indicating time, mood, and tenses.

Both Mong: Kuv   hu   nkauj (for three tenses)
English: I   sing   a   song (present tense)

I   sang   a   song (past tense)
I   will sing a   song (future tense)

Compared to English, Mong verbs do not take on various inflectional forms when indicating the tenses. However, this does not mean that the Mong do not have tenses. Tenses in Mong can usually be expressed by adverbial phrases.

Blue Mong: **Naagmo**, Kuv   hu nkauj (past tense)
White Hmong: **Naghmo**, Kuv   hu nkauj.
English: Yesterday, I   sang a song.

Blue Mong: **Nubnua**, Kuv   hu nkauj (present)
White Hmong: **Hnubno**, kuv   hu nkauj.
English: Today,   I   sing a song.

Blue Mong: **Pigkig**,   Kuv   hu nkauj (future)
Hmong Dawb: Tagkis,   Kuv   hu nkauj.
English: Tomorrow,   I will sing a song.

b) *Special Features of Verb Serialization in Mong*

In addition, there is a special feature in the sentence construction in Mong called "Verb serialization." In verb serialization, the Mong like to use two main verbs in one clause or in one sentence without using a conjunction to separate the two main verbs.

Blue Mong: Kuv   **moog ua** si.
White Hmong: Kuv   **mus   ua** si.
English: I   go do play.
--->   I   play.

Blue Mong: Kuv   **moog kawm** ntawv.
Hmong Dawb: Kuv   **mus   kawm** ntawv.
English: I   go learn   book.
--->   I   go to school.

Owensby called this special feature "Serial verbs." He asserted that the Mong verbs share this feature with Chinese languages.[32] This feature may cause some problems for Mong learners when they transfer the concept of verb serialization from Mong to English.

To sum up, Mong speaking students may have difficulties in the articulation of certain sounds in English, in the use of modal auxiliaries, and in verb formation as described in Section

8. Practical Suggestions for Classroom Teachers

Though Mong speaking students today were brought up in the United States, their parents maintain a balanced combination between Mong traditional life style and certain aspects of the mainstream of American culture. However, language barriers continue to impact the rate of adjustment for Mong speaking students particularly in the K-12 levels. Besides adjusting to the pressure of becoming academically proficient in the English language as well as the content areas, many Mong speaking students' level of English language proficiency is so limited that they cannot be placed in the mainstream classrooms. Though they may not have the same level of academic achievement compared to some other Asian-American students, they have had tremendous progress in the last two decades. If we are to solicit the many difficulty areas that Mong speaking students have, the list may be endless. However, the following contains some of the most difficult areas for them that mainstream teachers should be aware of in order to work with them during their acquisition of the English language. These areas of difficulties are summarized below:

1) Phonology

The Mong orthography was based on the Romanized Popular Alphabets (RPA). As a result, Mong consonantal phonemes contain a single, double, triple, as well as quadruple consonantal blends. Though there are more consonants in Mong than in English, they still have problems with the phonemic awareness and pronunciation with certain sounds in English. This includes:

a)   Initial sounds: /b/, /v/, /w/, /z/, /j/, /z/, /θ/, /t/, /ð/, /d/

b)   Consonantal clusters, e.g. corps   through

c)   All ending sounds, e.g. Plural and past tense allomorphs
     Plural allomorphs: /-s/, /-z/, /-∂z/
     Past tense allomorphs: /-d/, /-t/, /-∂d/

d)   Lax vowels, particularly the short vowels in English.

Similarly lax (short) vowels do not exist in Mong. This

also includes part of the prosodic suprasegmental features which are pitch, stress or accent, and intonation. The critical part involves the use of the lax (short) vowels in English, e.g.

/I/ as in bit   /ɛ/ as in bet
/æ/ as in bait   /U/ as in butt

e)   Vowe Digraphs, e.g.

t**oo**   t**wo**   thr**ough**   thr**ew**   cl**ue**   sh**oe**

The use of modal auxiliaries (helping verbs) as they relate to the semantics of English. It is recommended that modal auxiliaries be taught to Mong speaking students as part of their curricula. Be aware that the corresponding sounds in Mong and English are pronounced slightly differently due to their places and manners of articulation (See Table 25). One effective way to teach pronunciation is through the use of minimal pairs. For example, if Mong speaking students have problems pronouncing sounds, such as /r/, /v/, /θ/, /ð/, teachers should use minimal pairs to teach their Mong speaking students. They should begin to teach their students from the sounds that their students are familiar with to those unfamiliar, e.g.

lice/rice   fan/van   bath/bathe
/l/ --> /r/   /f/ --> /v/   /θ/ --> /ð/

2) Morphology

As discussed previously, Mong language is non-derivational compared to English. Teachers need to teach Mong speaking students the following concepts:

a) *Pronunciation of all ending sounds*

Mong lexicons generally end with tone markers and the Mong do not pronounce the ending sounds; whereas in English the inflectional morphemes are pronounced. Because derivational morphology does not exist in Mong, teachers may need to constantly remind the Mong speaking students that all lexical words in English endings are pronounced. There may be times that teachers may need to exaggerate the endings so that their students can hear the ending sounds. Teachers may, from time to time, help their students to break the polysyllabic words in English into syllables and morphemes so that their students can assign the syllables and morphemes to those that correspond to the Mong lexicons.

b) The Concepts of Affixes in English

Because Mong language is considered non-derivational, the use of affixes (prefixes and suffixes and root morphemes) is foreign to Mong speaking students. Teaching the concepts of affixes will help Mong speaking students augment their lexicons, their vocabulary development and their comprehension, which is an essential part of language development.

c) The Concept of Subcategorization in English

Subcategorization is defined as the part of the lexical entry of a lexicon that specifies which syntactic categories can and cannot occur with it in a sentence, e.g.

- to be interested in something (interested is always followed by the preposition in)
- to be fond of something (to be fond is always followed by the preposition of)

d) The Use of Suppletive Forms (or Suppletions)

Suppletive forms or suppletions are the exceptions to the rule, e.g. the plural forms of the following words, that do not follow the regular plural rule:

man/men	fish/fish	deer
woman/women	child/children	deer

3) Syntax

a) Use of Inflected Forms as in Tense, Gender, and Cases

Though Mong language follows the English sentence patterns of Subject + Verb + Object (SVO), syntax may be one of the most difficult areas for Mong speaking students. Mong words do not carry any inflected forms, such as the plural, possessive of nouns, genders, and cases of pronouns (me, I, mine) and the tenses (including present, past, gerund, past participle, progressive form). Because there are so many tenses in English, the use of the appropriate tenses for Mong speaking students may be very difficult for them to master the concepts. Therefore, teachers may want to be aware of this area of difficulty.

b) *Word Order*

Word order in Mong follows the pattern of English, except for adjectives. In English, adjectives normally precede nouns; whereas in Mong, adjectives are situated after the nouns that they modify, e.g.

Mong: <u>lub   tsev   ntsuab</u>
         (clf.)   house green
English: a   green   house

c) *Serial Verb Construction*

Teachers may need to observe that Mong speaking students may use a series of verbs that are strung together in the same sentence. This is the result of language transfer of the serial verb construction in Mong to English introduced earlier in this chapter.

4) Semantics

Semantics is described as the study of meanings of language so that an individual can make sense out of the words that are strung together to derive to a meaning. This may include the use of homonyms, synonyms (including polysemous words, like man and boy), and antonyms. Semantics may be one of the most difficult areas for Mong speaking students. Some of the most typical difficulties in this area are highlighted as follows:

a) *The Use of Idioms and Metaphors*

Idioms are expressions that tend to be frozen in forms and violate the syntactic rules, e.g.

once in a blue moon   for the time being
give a hand   making ends meet

Metaphors are expressions that do not take on the literal meaning of the sentences, e.g.

The sea never sleeps.
The walls have ears.

b) *The Use of Indefinite Articles (a and an) and Definite Article (the)*

Many students may take this for granted when it comes to the use of articles. Mong speaking students may not know how to differentiate the use of indefinite and definite articles. Mainstream teachers having Mong speaking students in their classrooms may want to elicit this as one of the most difficult areas for Mong students.

To sum up, Mong speaking students may have difficulties in the areas of phonology, morphology, syntax, and semantics. However, their difficulties tend to surround the lack of inflections, including tense, gender, noun classifiers, and serial verb construction. These difficulties may also vary from individual student to student depending upon the length of time since their arrival to the United States and the degree of their exposure to the English language, both at home and at school. Nevertheless, teachers may encounter Mong students who know neither Mong well, nor English well.

Summary

Chapter 6 provided a brief historical background of the Mong, the historical development of the Mong orthography, information on the characteristics of the Mong learners, a comparative discussion on the similarities and differences between the two Mong regional dialects. They included the Blue Mong and White Hmong. Then, a comparison between the two Mong dialects to the English language was made. This comparison encompasses in the areas of phonology, morphology, syntax, and semantics. This chapter concludes with some of the most difficult problems for Mong speaking students when they acquire English. The author hopes that this information will be helpful to mainstream teachers to be used as a resource to assist their Mong speaking students in their classrooms.

Chapter 7 contains an open letter with recommendations to the Mong, to their children, to local school districts and institutions of higher education, to the United States government, and to the state and local governments.

Notes

[1] California Department of Education, Language Census (Sacramento, CA: California Department of Education, 1997).

[2] Anthony Arlotto, *Introduction to Historical Linguistics* (Lanham, MD: University Press of America, Inc., 1972), p. 52.

[3] K. Chang, *The Reconstruction of Proto Miao-Yao Tones BIHP* (Berkeley, CA: University of California and Academia Sinica, 1972.

[4] F. Michael, *China Through the Ages: History of a Civilization* (Boulder, CO: Westview Press, 1986), p. 18-43.

[5] William A. Smalley, *Linguistic Diversity and National Unity: Language Ecology in Thailand* (Chicago, IL: The University of Chicago Press, 1994).

[6] Samuel Pollard, *The Story of the Miao* (London: Henry Hooks, 1919), p. 173) and William H. Hudspeth, *Stone-Gateway and the Flowery Miao* (London: The Cargate Press, 1937), p. 173).

[7] Ibid., Pollard, p. 173 & 185.

[8] Paoze Thao, Mong Resettlement in the Chicago Area (1978-1987): Educational Implications, Ph.D. Dissertation, Loyola University of Chicago, 1994; and *Kevcai Siv Lug Moob* [Foundations of Mong Language] (Marina, CA: PT Publishing, 1997).

[9] Ibid.; Thao, 1994 and 1997.

[10] Ibid.; Thao, 1994 and 1997.

[11] Ibid.; Thao, 1994 and 1997.

[12] George L. Barney, Christianity: Innovation in Meo Culture, MA Thesis, University of Minnesota, 1957, p. 68.

[13] William A. Smalley, "History of the Development of the Hmong Romanized Popular Alphabet," Presentation and Handout to the Hmong Language Council, Minneapolis, MN at the University of Minnesota, August 12, 1982.

[14] William A. Smalley, "The Problems of Consonants and Tone: Hmong (Meo, Miao), "*Phonemes and Orthography: Language Planning in Ten Minority Languages of Thailand* (Canberra, Australia: Australian National University, 1976, 4: 85-123.

[15] Ibid.; Thao, 1994 and 1997.

[16] Ibid.; Smalley, 1976 and 1994.

[17] Bruce T. Bliatout; Bruce Downing; Judy Lewis; and Dao Yang, *Handbook for Teaching Hmong-Speaking Students* (Folsom, CA: Folsom Cordova Unified School District, Southeast Asia Community Resource Center, 1988).

[18] W.R. Geddes, Migrants of the Mountains: The Cultural Ecology of the Blue Miao (Hmong Njua) of Thailand (Oxford: Clarendon Press, 1976).

[19] P. Giglioli, *Language and Social Context* (New York, N.Y.: Penguin Books, 1972.

[20] H. Purnell, Toward a Reconstruction of Proto Miao-Yao, Ph.D. Dissertation, Cornell University, 1970; and William Smalley, "The Problems of Consonants and Tone: Hmong (Meo, Miao)," *Phonemes and Orthography: Language Planning in Ten Minority Language of Thailand* (Canberra, Australia: Australian National University, 1976), 4:85-123.

[21] Ibid.; Smalley, 1994, p. 245.

[22] Ibid.; Smalley, 1976, p. 98-99.
[23] Ibid.; Purnell, 1970; and Smalley, 1976 and 1994.
[24] Ibid.; Thao, 1994, p. 15.
[25] Keith Quincy, *Hmong: History of a People* (Cheney, Washington: Eastern Washington University Press, 1988), p. 32.
[26] Ibid.; 1997, p. 13.
[27] Ibid.; Fromkin and Rodman, 1998, p. 236-237 and 280.
[28] Ibid.; Fromkin and Rodman, 1998, p. 531.
[29] National Clearinghouse, General Information Series #15, "The Hmong Language: Sentences, Phrases, and Words" (Arlington, VA: Center for Applied Linguistics, 1978), p. 6.
[30] Ibid.; Fromkin and Rodman, 1998, p. 219.
[31] Paoze Thao, Teaching Modals in Mong ESL Classes, MA Departmental Paper, Northeastern Illinois University, Unpublished Paper, 1985.
[32] Ibid.; Bliatout et al, 1988, p. 56.

Chapter 7

An Open Letter

Coming from a rural background, the Mong experienced tremendous frustration during the initial resettlement period in the United States from 1978-1987. Their lives and education had been totally disrupted by the US Secret War in Laos which was a part of the Vietnam Conflict. The Mong were illiterate in their own language. Their lack of formal education in Laos makes it difficult for them to earn a living in a technologically-developed country, such as the United States. The language barrier impeded development of their full potentialities and their becoming contributing members in the society. Their difficult adjustment consequently resulted in their massive secondary migration from one city to another, from one state to another, e.g. from Chicago (Illinois) to Fresno (California), Green Bay (Wisconsin), and Minneapolis and St. Paul (Minnesota).

What should be done if there is a similar challenge in the future regarding refugee resettlement? In order for the Mong or similar groups to have a smooth transition to new lives in the United States, the author writes this open letter with specific recommendations addressed directly to the Mong or similar groups, to Mong students or their children, to the Voluntary Agencies (VOLAGs), to the local school districts, to institutions of higher education, and to federal, state and local government agencies involved.

To the Mong

Many factors, delineated in earlier chapters, may have held the Mong back from fully acculturating to the mainstream and diverse cultures in the United States. However, two factors are critical and stand out above others. The first factor relates to the language barrier that has decelerated their rate of adjustment. The second one deals with their attitudes that held them back even further.

1. Language Barrier

Some Mong are still longing to return to their homeland. In the past two decades, the Mong people were influenced by two forms of political leadership. The former influenced many Mong to return to Laos to fight the Communists. The latter focused on community building and development for permanent resettlement in the United States.

The author recommends that each individual Mong-American needs to start taking control of their own destiny by focusing on the present and the future rather than the past. The author recognizes that nobody would help them unless they help themselves. The Mong should plan short and long-term objectives for their lives. They should design specific plans of action to become economically self-sufficient as soon as possible. The Mong leadership at each locality should encourage small-scale economic development projects such as grocery stores, restaurants, and other small businesses that may be achievable and profitable for the Mong. The aim is to develop self-esteem for the Mong community. However, the real goals must be determined by each individual Mong. The language barrier might be overcome if one keeps trying on a continuing basis.

2. Attitude Adjustment

Changing the Mong's attitudes could be one of the most challenging tasks in their lives. The older the person, the deeper the attachment to their motherland. It is very difficult to erase their memories and to detach them from their motherland. However, the author suggests that the Mong should focus on the present and the future. They should embrace the United States as their country and do their best to become contributing members in this society. They should move forward toward the future.

Culturally, the Mong should conform to the host culture by not practicing certain customs such as polygamy, "*Yuav Nam Tij*" (a Mong custom where the next younger brother of a deceased brother marries his sister-in-law, becomes the step father and cares for his deceased brother's children), abduction of girls for wives (forced marriage), and early marriages. These Mong customs are not acceptable and in some cases, illegal, in the United States.

On the other hand, the Mong should preserve certain aspects of their culture such as the notion of respect for the elderly, for their family and their culture, the importance of the clan system, folktales, crafts, arts, and music to sustain their cultural existence and to meet their human needs. These particular aspects of the Mong culture are incomparable to what one could find in the various cultures in the United States. These cultural characteristics are worth to preserve and make the Mong community unique. In other words, the Mong should be able to make selective adaptation and know how to balance between their culture and the cultures of the diverse ethno-cultural groups in the United States. In other words, they should be able to balance between the process of enculturation (learning the patterns of their own culture) and acculturation (learning how to adjust to other cultures without giving up the Mong culture). This is very critical to the survival of the Mong ethno-cultural identity in the United States.

In terms of community building, the rise and the fall of several Mong Mutual Assistance Associations (MAAs) throughout the nation have taught the Mong a very important lesson. The Mong should study the western notion of the voluntary organizations relative to the roles of the board of directors, methods, and staff selection. They should stay out of controversial issues (such as jealousy, misconception, misjudgment, status of leadership, the gender issue between men and women for example) that have been embedded deeply in the Mong communities since the turn of century. *Robert's Rules of Order* should be implemented at all times when conducting meetings for the purpose of achieving constructive and effective results. They need to work to create a vision statement for their organizations that is inclusive of all the Mong, to organize long-term planning, and to devise strategic and specific plans of actions for implementation. Past experience demonstrates that the board of directors often wasted too much time or used time unproductively in meetings. They need to stay focused with the meeting agenda.

The Mong should be united rather than divided into factions because they have interdependent needs. Though some of these MAAs were dissolved, new self-help organizations should be re-established to assist the Mong people to build their new lives throughout the United States. The Mong should keep in mind that forming mutual self-help or not-for-profit organizations requires solid knowledge and a good understanding of organization, and the process coupling with both personal and professional commitment, persistence and a global vision for the welfare of the whole community. Past experiences illustrate that a few individuals in the Mong community has politicized the process to promote self-interest and personal gains. This politicization of the MAAs only makes the matter worse in the Mong community.

The best guarantee for peaceful co-existence between Mong groups and/or between the Mong and other groups is for the Mong to respect, recognize, and allow diversity, be it linguistic, religious, and racial. Fragmentation along socio-linguistic, religious, political or other lines for personal or family gain can plant the seeds for senseless conflict in the Mong communities in the years to come. The Mong should nurture, preserve, and respect their diversity and differences and not risk the prospect of dissension and cultural incompatibility which can develop into serious problems within the Mong society. Besides these internal factors, the Mong should be aware of the external factors, such as the local and state government's intervention in their community affairs. The Mong should now redefine themselves as a community within a larger nation-state such as the United States.

The author wants to stress the importance of becoming American citizens by encouraging Mong to become politically involved at the local, state, and federal levels in order to have a greater impact on legislation at the local, state and national levels. The Mong should be determined, honest, and practical in bringing their voices and concerns to the local, state, and federal governments. Specific issues that affect the Mong domestically and internationally could be addressed to the local, state and federal governments through this channel, e.g. issues involving the forced repatriation of the Mong refugees in Thailand and other countries and the use of chemical warfare against the Mong in Laos by the Soviet Union, etc.

Educationally, Mong parents should keep in mind that teachers in the United States are not "second parents" as they have anticipated. They should pay attention to the education of their children. They should have their children involved in extra-curricular activities, such as church programs for youth, Young Men's Christian Associations (YMCA) swimming programs, Boys or Girls' Scouts' programs, American Youth Soccer Organizations (AYSO) programs, etc. These are activities that would focus their children's attention on developing positive attitudes toward society. It is important that Mong parents are aware of the availability of these programs, get their children involved in these activities and take the leadership to actively participate in these programs. They should recognize that learning is a lifelong process.

Mong parents who still depend on welfare utilization should continue to take English classes on a continuing basis. This may be the only means to overcome the language barrier. English language proficiency is the key to their successful acculturation to the mainstream culture and new life in the United States. As soon as they learn English, the Mong should look for jobs. By becoming economically self-supportive, they could set a good example for their children. This action will influence and will instill the value of diligence, hard work, familial and social responsibility in their children. The sense of work ethics and social responsibility begins with a good understanding of the self and deviates to the family, community, the nation and the world or vice-versa from an interdependent world, to the nation, to a community, to family, and then to self.

The action of finding employment alone will not address all the problems of the Mong community. Many Mong have secured fulfilling employment in the United States. However, some of these families became "workaholics" and paid less attention to the academic progress of their children in school. No parents in the family had time to instill the moral character and social values in their children. As a result, their children did not know where to draw the line between right and wrong as they grew up with the influence of peer pressure. The author recommends that Mong parents should spend more time nurturing and educating their children. Besides parenting, they should orient their children with career goals and should provide them with sufficient school supplies and clothing. They should encourage their children to develop to their full potential. Both Mong parents need to support their children, reinforce and monitor their children's progress at schools. For single parent families, though these roles may not be fulfilled, they could be substituted for someone like uncles, the head of household, or the clan leaders.

By following up with their children's daily activities, they could identify and seek solutions to their children's problems before they become serious. The Mong should develop strategies to prevent early marriages. Mong parents should counsel and advise their daughters to continue their higher education and seek certain occupational skills prior to starting their own families. Schooling should be stressed in family life. In this manner, preventative mechanisms could be devised to keep their children away from gangs, pre-marital sex, drugs, and, to a certain extent, peer pressure.

To Mong Students

Mong students at the elementary and secondary school levels should learn how to cope with acclimation. The following concepts that the author proposes for Mong students are analogous to American values. Mong students should not become "Americanized" too soon. Rapid Americanization could be prevented through learning how to preserve certain positive aspects of Mong culture and learn how to balance between the enculturation and the acculturation process between the Mong and mainstream cultures.

Mong students should avoid the intergeneration gap and peer pressure. Recognizing that they are Mong-Americans, they should learn how to make a selective adaptation to the American culture in order to withstand peer pressure. They should obey their parents by safeguarding certain positive aspects of the Mong culture, e.g. the concept of respect, the importance of the clan system, the values of family and extended families, and the life of a community.

At the higher educational level, Mong students should study as diligently as their American counterparts and should spend even more time on their studies. They should not hesitate to ask their faculty for more assistance. In addition, they should develop study habits and strategies that would help them in their studies and research. They should initiate some types of Mong student clubs at various institutions of higher learning to address their concerns to the universities. These clubs could be used as a center to keep the Mong students informed about the various resources of the universities that are available to them and as a bridge between the universities and the Mong students. However, the ultimate goal of these clubs should be for Mong students to provide leadership in the area of academic support for their members so that they could graduate from the universities. Mong students could utilize the clubs for the purpose of tutoring and advising one another about course selection. Occasionally, faculty members could be invited to participate and present to members of the so that they will be familiarized themselves Mong students. In this manner, faculty and alumni may provide students with insight and orientation on specific topics that may be beneficial to everyone in the club.

To School Districts and Institutions of Higher Learning

The author recommends that school districts should provide a bilingual and bicultural approach to learning. Districts should not immerse Mong students or other recent immigrant groups into the monolingual English classrooms immediately (known as "Sink or Swim" model without providing any primary language instructional support. After that, they should be immersed when they are ready. Several steps may be provided and may be taken by school districts during this transitional period as follows:

1. Adequacy of Bilingual Staff

Adequate bilingual staff support would be very beneficial to Mong students in order for them to make a smooth transition from the elementary school level to the secondary school level. The trained bilingual and bicultural staff with linguistic and cultural knowledge of the Mong appear to be one of the most effective approaches in educating the Mong. The bilingual staff may seek to ameliorate the cultural and educational problems, teaching and learning as well as the acculturation process for the Mong students.

2. Acquisition of Bilingual Cross-Cultural, Language Academic Development (BCLAD) or Cross-Cultural, Language Academic Development (CLAD) teachers

School districts should make every attempt to employ teachers who have been trained in the Cross-cultural, Language Academic Development (CLAD) or Bilingual Cross-cultural, Language Academic Development (BCLAD) to teach the Mong students. Pre-service teachers with the appropriate teacher preparation training programs in CLAD and BCLAD could also facilitate a smooth transition for Mong students as well.

3. Services from Committed Staff

Mong students could also benefit from services from para-educators or paraprofessionals with a combination of skills and training from various disciplines. The author believes that there are many effective ways to educate the Mong students. The staff do not have to be a Mong in order to deliver effective approaches to the Mong. The most critical consideration lies with the staff who have a deep commitment and a passion for their profession and who are willing to go out of their way to make things happen for the Mong students. In fact, education cuts across and beyond ethnic, political, racial, and socio-economic lines. The author believes that any educator with this deep commitment can make a big difference in the future lives of many Mong students so that they will become moral and contributing members in the society.

At the higher educational level, faculty, staff and administrators should be sensitive to the needs of Mong students and provide them assistance as they see appropriate and needed in order for the

Mong students to make it through college. Special programs should be instituted in various institutions of higher learning and may be staffed with bilingual Mong-American staff to mentor, coach and nurture them for academic success in their programs.

For adult education, comprehensive Adult English as a Second Language (ESL) should be developed immediately to teach English to Mong adults on a continuing basis. In many places, English language training for Mong was not developed until the 1980's due to the lack of financial resources at the federal, state and local educational institutions. Those refugees who arrived between 1975 and 1980 had little English language training. Those Mong refugees who arrived after 1980 did not speak English and were required to attend more English language lessons before they were ready for job placement.

The author suggests that pilot projects and more research should be conducted at the local levels heavily impacted by the Mong and other recent immigrants. The objectives of these pilot projects should be to research the various specific methods of instruction that are effective for this unique Mong adult learners. The author believes that the effective methods for Adult ESL classes should include lessons with hands-on focusing on the reality of work. Instructors should stay away from classroom discussions due to their limited knowledge of the English language. Mong adults are not used to the teaching styles that require a lot of group discussion aimed to achieve their communicative competence during their initial stage of language acquisition. Forcing Mong adult students to produce functional English could only add more distress and disturbance to their learning process. In other words, they should be taught in self-contained classrooms before they are placed in mixed settings with any other language groups. Of course, the curriculum should incorporate the bilingual and bicultural approach to learning. Lessons should be organized and should be taught thematically in a chronological and sequential order before implementing them in the classrooms. Thao's study in 1994 indicated between 1978-1987 the idea of integrating different language groups at various levels of ability in the same classrooms at the beginning of adult ESL program runs the risk of many dropping out of the program. Those who learned fast often become bored and those who were slower could not keep up the pace and often dropped out. [1]

To the United States Federal Government

The federal government has a long-term moral and financial obligation to assist the Mong in their long-term resettlement in the

United States. After all, the entire generation of the Mong in the United States today was involved in the U.S. Secret war in Laos. The Mong have specific problems that need special attention. The Highland Lao Initiative project was a perfect example. However, the project was too short in duration and received too few resources to sustain its programs for a longer period. This demonstrated that the federal government lacked a firm commitment in the development of a comprehensive and concrete plan for the long-term successful Mong resettlement in the United States.

The federal government knew ahead of time that thousands of the Southeast Asian refugees would have come to the United States prior to 1975. The federal government could have developed a concrete plan and could have collaborated with the local and state governments and the public and private sectors to prepare for the massive influx of refugees from Southeast Asia. Although Southeast Asian refugees came to the United States since 1975, they were left under the care and responsibility of the local VOLAGs, private American sponsors and church groups. This put a tremendous burden on the local and state governments and private American sponsors and the local churches. It took almost five years before Congress finally passed the Refugee Act of 1980 to allocate funding to assist in their adjustment to the new country. The United States government could have done a better job by providing sufficient financial resources to local school districts to accommodate the process of resettlement for these thousands of refugees.

Additional concrete plans could have been devised at the federal level with the collaboration from the state and local governments and private and public sectors, the local grassroots organizations to get involved for the successful implementation of the refugee programs. Past experiences have demonstrated that the federal government only responded to crisis. Once the crisis is over, the federal government drops the case. This demonstrates that the federal government lacks of a long term commitment to the solution of problems. We may never know all the consequences that the Southeast Asian refugees have faced during this difficult transition. The Southeast Asian refugees have in fact suffered tremendous consequences as a result of poor planning from the federal government. For example, it took thousand of Mong refugee families to move to the Central Valley of California before the federal government realized that the Mong refugees had problems and need some attention. Remember that Southeast Asian refugees were already resettled in the United States since 1975, but the Refugee Act passed in Congress in 1980. It took five years before Congress pass the Refugee Acts of 1980 into law. What happened during those five years. The Refugee Education Assistance Act (REAC) was also passed into law in 1980. Prior to that, the local and state governments had to pick up the cost for educating refugees. Educators knew well in advance that there would be a massive immigration of refugees into this country. However, the politicians and the bureaucrats did not provide the educators any significant financial resources until the refugee children started to flood the school system in massive numbers.

To the State and Local Governments

After all of these problems, the author would like to caution the state and local government. Sometimes the state and local government officials do not have any sensitivity to the socio-linguistic, ethno-cultural and religious differences in the Mong community. Instead of doing the Mong communities some good, they just escalate the problems into crisis. The state and local governments should stay out of the natural Mong leadership development process. Their intrusion into the internal affairs of the Mong Mutual Assistance Associations (MAAs) only created a skeptical attitude from the Mong leaders toward the state and local government not just in the local and state that are involved but throughout the nation. Because the close-knit of the Mong communities in the nation, problems occur in a particular Mong community between local, state and federal government officials travel fast to the various Mong communities in the United States.

Summary

In conclusion, the Mong, coming from a semi-traditional life style, adjusted amazingly well in a highly technological society such as the United States. Though the Mong culture was diametrically different from that of the United States, the freedom guaranteed under the US Constitution poses no threat to their identity in contrast to their forced integration into a dominant culture like China. They have the right to adapt, adopt, preserve, and maintain their ethnic identity as Mong-Americans.

The future of the Mong depends on education. The younger generation of the Mong has enhanced opportunity for socio-economic mobility. Known for their intelligence, adaptability, and love for freedom, the Mong continue to adjust as a community. Through hard work, determination, and perseverance, the young Mong are expected to successfully acculturate into the American society. The Mong will advance to their full potential and contribute greatly to the advancement of life in the United States.

Notes

[1] Paoze Thao, Mong Resettlement in the Chicago Area (1978-1987): Educational Implications. Ph.D. Dissertation, Loyola University of Chicago, 1994.

BIBLIOGRAPHY

Abraham, May. "Assyrian Ethnicity in Education in Chicago." ED.D. Dissertation, Loyola University of Chicago, 1984.

Aponte, G. D. "The Enigma of Bangungut," *Annals of Internal Medicine.* 52:1258-1263.

Arlotto, Anthony. *Introduction to Historical Linguistics.* U.S.A.: University Press of America, Inc., 1972.

Barney, George L. "Christianity: Innovation in Meo Cutlure." MA Thesis, University of Minnesota, 1957.

Barney, George L. "The Hmong of Northern Laos." Arlington: National Clearinghouse, Center for Applied Linguistics, General Information #16, n.d.

Barney, George L. and Smalley, William A. "Third Report on Meo (Miao): Orthography and Grammar." Mimeo, 1953.

Bender, Sharon Rae. "Soviet Immigrant Jewry in the Chicago Area (1960-1980): Enculturation and Education." Ph.D. Dissertation, Loyola University of Chicago, 1992.

Berger, Carl. *The United States Air Force in Southeast Asia.* Washington, D.C.: Office of Air Force History, 1977.

Bernatzik, Hugo Adolf. *Akha and Miao.* New Haven: Human Relations Area Files, Inc., 1970.

Binney, G.A. *The Social and Economic Organization of Two White Meo Communities in Thailand.* Washington: Advanced Research Program Agency, 1968.

Bitters, Barbara A. and Staff of Equity & Multicultural Education Section, "Pupil Population in Wisconsin Public Schools Protected by Pupil Nondiscrimination Provisions. Madison, Wisconsin: Wisconsin Department of Public Instruction, November 1993.

Bliatout, Bruce Thowpaow. *Hmong Sudden Unexpected Nocturnal Death Syndrome: A Cultural Study.* Portland: Sparkle Publishing Enterprises, 1982.

Boulding, Elise. *Building a Global Civic Culture: Education for an Interdependent World.* New York: Teachers College Press, 1988.

Branfman, Frederic. *Voices from the Plain of Jars: Life under an Air War.* New York: Harper Colophon Books, 1972.

Bruchett, Wilfred G. *The Second Indochina War: Cambodia and Laos.* New York: International Publishers, 1970.

Burutphat, Khachatphay. *Chone Kloum Noi Nai Thai Kup Khouame Mane Khong Khaun Chat* [Minorities in Thailand and National Security]. Bangkok: Praie Pittaya Publishing, Co., B.E. 2526 (1983), pp. 277-315.

California Department of Education. Language Census. Sacramento, CA: California Department of Education, 1995 and 1998.

Chamot, Anna Uhl. Changing Instruction for Language Minority Students to Achieve National Goals," *Proceedings of the Third National Research Symposium on Limited English Proficient Student Issues: Focus on Middle and High School* Issues. Vol. 1. Washington, D.C.: U.S. Department of Education, Office of Bilingual Education and Minority Languages Affairs, 1993.

Center for Applied Linguistics. *The Peoples and Cultures of Cambodia,Laos, and Vietnam.* Washington, D.C.: Center for Applied Linguistics, 1981.

Chafe, William A. *The Unfinished Journey.* New York: Oxford Press, 1968.

Chang, Kun. *The Reconstruction of Proto-Miao-Yao Tones BIHP.* Berkeley: University of California and Academia Sinica, 1972.

Coombs, Philip H. *The World Crisis in Education: The View from the Eighties.* New York: Oxford University Press, 1985.

Dengler, Dieter. *Escape from Laos.* San Rafael: Presidio Press, 1979.

Energy, Poverty, and Refugee Services. "Known Indochinese Refugee Population in Wisconsin." Madison, Wisconsin: Wisconsin Department of Health and Human Services, June 1994.

Evenrud, Carole J. An Educator's Response to Southeast Asian Street Gangs. MA Thesis,   Hamline University, 1992.

Friedman, Joan et al. *Working with Refugees: A Manual for Paraprofessionals. Vol. III, Intercultural   Counseling and Interviewing Skills.* Chicago, Illinois: Travelers Aid/ Immigrants Service, 1981.

Fromkin, Victoria and Rodman, Robert. *An Introduction to Language.* 6th Ed. Fort Worth, TX: Harcourt Brace College Publishers, 1998.

Garrett, W. E. "The Hmong of Laos: No Place to Run," *National Geographic,* Vol. No. 1. Washington,D.C.: NationalGeographic Society. January 1974, pp. 78-111.

Geddes, W. R. *Migrants of the Mountains: The Cultural Ecology of the Blue Miao (Hmong Njua) of Thailand.* Oxford: Clarendon Press, 1976.

Giglioli, P. *Language and Social Context.* New York, NY: Penguin Books, 1972.

Goza, Franklin William. "Adjustment and Adaptation among Southeast Asian Refugees in the United States." Ph.D. Dissertation, University of Wisconsin, Madison, 1987.

Gutek, Gerald L. *A History of the Western Educational Experience.* Prospect Heights: Waveland Press, Inc., 1972.

Hamilton-Merritt. "Tragic Legacy from Laos," *The Reader's Digest,* August 1981, pp. 96- 100.

Hanhoe, Ruth. *Contemporary Chinese Education.* Armonk: M. E. Sharpe, Inc., 1984.

Haudricourt, A. G. *Problàmes de Pholologie Diachronique.* Paris, France: Centre National de la Recherche Scientifique, 1972.

Jankowski, Martin Sanchez. *Islands in the Street: Gangs and American Urban Society.* Berkeley, CA: University of California Press, 1991.

Lyman, Thomas Amis. *Grammar of Mong Njua (Green Miao): A Descriptive Linguistic Study.* Sattley, CA: Published by the Author, The Blue Oak Press, 1979.

Human Relations Area Files. *Laos: its People, its Society, its Culture.* New Haven: Hraf Press, 1960.

Jewish Federation of Metropolitan Chicago. Annual Report for the Year Ended June 30, 1989: Refugee Entrant Social Services Program. Chicago: Jewish Federation of Metropolitan Chicago, 1989, Appendix B - Committee Lists.

Koschmann, Nancy L. and Tobin, Joseph J. *Working with Indochinese Refugees: A Handbook for Mental Health and Human Service Providers.* Chicago: Travelers Aid/Immigrants' Service League of Chicago, n.d.

Lao Royal Ordinance of 1962, No. 648, n.d.

Larteguy, Jean. *La Fabuleuse Aventure du Peuple de l'Opium.* Paris: Presses de la Cite, 1979.

Lee, Chae-Jin. *Communist China's Policy toward Laos: A Case Study, 1954-67.* Lawrence, Kansas: Center for East Asian Studies, University of Kansas, 1970.

Lewis, James H. *A Profile of the Cambodian, Laotian, and Vietnamese People in the United States.* Chicago, Illinois: NAFEA, March 1994)

Lewis, Paul and Lewis, Elaine. *Peoples of the Golden Triangle: Six Tribes in Thailand.* London: Thames and Hudson, Ltd., 1984, pp. 100-133.

Quincy, Keith. *Hmong: History of a People.* Cheney: Eastern Washington University Press, 1988 and 1994.

Magill, Frank N. *Magill's Cinema Annual 1985: A Survey of 1984 Films.* Englewood Cliffs, N.J.: Salem Press, 1985.

Marshall, Eliot. "The Hmong: Dying and Cultural Shock?," *Science.* Vol. 12, 1981, pp. 22-23.

McInnis, Kathleen M.; Petracchi, Helen E.; and Morgenbesser, Mel. *The Hmong in America: Providing Ethnic-Sensitive Health, Education, and Human Services.* Dubuque: Kendall/Hunt Publishing Company, 1990.

Mickey, P. M. *The Cowrie Shell Miao of Kweichow.* Cambridge: Peabody Museum of American Archaeology, 1947.

Mottin, Jean. *The History of the Hmong (Meo).* Bangkok: Odeon Store, Ltd., 1980.

Munger, Ronald G. "Sudden Adult Death in Asian Population: The Case of the Hmong," *The Hmong in the West.* Ed. Minneapolis: University of Minnesota, 1982, pp. 307-319.

Neuenschwander, John A. *Oral History: As a Teaching Approach.* Washington, D.C.: National Education Association of the United States, 1976.

152   *Bibliography*

Nolan, Keith William. *Into Laos: Dewey Canyon II/Lam Son 719.* Novato, California: Presidio Press, 1986.

North, David S.; Finck, John; Downing, Bruce; Thao, Paoze; Vang, Shoua; and Yang, Teng. *An Evaluation of the Highland Lao Initiative.* Washington, D.C.: Office of Refugee Resettlement, U.S. Department of Health and Human Services, 1985.

North, David S.; Lewin, Lawrence S.; and Wagner, Jennifer R. *Kaleidoscope: The Resettlement of Refugees in the U.S. by the Voluntary Agencies.* Washington, D.C.: New TransCentury Foundation, Lewin and Associates, and National Opinion Research Center, 1982.

North, David S. and Yang, Doua. *Profiles of the Highland Lao Communities in the United States.* Washington, D.C.: Office of Refugee Resettlement, U.S. Department of Health and Human Services, 1988.

Noss, Richard. *Higher Education and Development in Southeast Asia.* Vol. III Part 2: Language Policy and Higher Education. Paris: United Nations Educational, Scientific and Cultural Organizations, and the International Association of Universities, 1967, VIII: 123.

Oalmann, M. C. "Sudden Death, Coronary Heart Disease, Atherosclerosis and Myocardial Lesion in Young Men," *American Journal of Epidemiology.* 112 (5): 308-310.

Outsama, Kao. "Educational Administration in Laos," *Bulletin of the UNESCO Office for Education in Asia, No. 15, Administration of Education in the Asian Region.* Bangkok:UNESCO, 1974, pp. 115-128.

Policies and Procedures of the "Chicago Resettlement Demonstration Project." Chicago: Catholic Charities, Illinois Conference of Churches, Jewish Family and Community Service, Lutheran Child and Family Service, Travelers and Immigrants Aid, and World Relief Corporation, 1985.

Prendergast, Nancy E. "A Vietnamese Refugee Family in the United States from 1975-1985: A Case Study." Ph.D. Dissertation, Loyola University of Chicago, 1985.

Provo, G. *Laos: Programmes et Manuel Scolaires.* UNESCO, No. de serie: 1255/BMS.RD/EDM. Paris: UNESCO, 1969.

Ratliff, Martha Susan. The Morphological Functions of Tone in White Hmong. Ph.D. Dissertation, University of Chicago, 1986.

Reder, Stephen. *The Hmong Resettlement Study.* Final Report, Vol. 1. Washington, D.C.: U.S. Department of Health and Human Services, 1985.

Reed, Tipawan Truong-Quang. "The Hmong Highlanders and the Lao Lowlanders." Chicago: Governor's Center for Asian Assistance, May 1978, 4-7.

Refugee Mutual Assistance Associations. Joint Letter to the United States Department of State. Chicago, Illinois. 10 September 1984.

Regional Institute of Higher Education and Development. *Proceedings of the Workshop Held in Singapore 26-29 July 1971.* Singapore, September 1971, p. 37.

Roberts, T. D; Carroll, Mary Elizabeth; Kaplan, Irving; Matthew, Jan M.; McMorris, David S.; and Townsend, Charles. *Area Handbook for Laos*. Washington, D.C.: U.S. Government Printing Office, 1967.

Robbins, Christopher. *The Ravens: The Men Who Flew in America's Secret War in Laos*. New York: Crown Publisher, Inc., 1978.

Savina, F. M. *Histoire des Miao*. Paris: Societe des Missions Etrangeres, 1924.

Schanche, Don A. *Mister Pop*. New York: David McKay Company, Inc., 1970.

Scott, George M. "A New Year in a New Land: Religious Change among the Lao Hmong Refugees in San Diego," *The Hmong in the West*. Ed. Minneapolis: University of   Minnesota, 1982, pp. 63-81.

Seying, James. Letter to author, 28 December 1992.

Shaplen, Robert. *Time out of Hand: Revolution and Reaction in Southeast Asia*. New York: Harper & Row, Publishers, 1962.

Sherman, Spencer. "The Hmong in America: Laotian Refugees in the Land of the Giants," *National Geographic*. Vol. 174, No. 4. Washington, D.C.: National Geographic Society, October 1978, pp. 587-610.

Smalley, William A. ed. "The Problems of Consonants and Tone: Hmong (Meo, Miao)," *Phonemes and Orthography: Language Planning in Ten Minority Languages of Thailand*. Canberra: Australian National University, 4: 85-123.

Smalley, William A. "History of the Development of the Mong Literacy," Presentation to the Hmong Language Council. University of Minnesota, 12 August 1982.

Smalley, William A. *Linguistic Diversity and National Unity: Language Ecology in Thailand*. Chicago: The University of Chicago Press, 1994.

Souvannaphouma, Prince Mangkra. *L'Agonie du Laos*. Plon: Presse de la Simped, 1975.

Tate, D. J. M. *The making of Modern South-East Asia*. Vol. I. Kualalumpur: Oxford University Press, 1971, pp. 487-495.

Thao, Cheu and Robson, Barbara. *Interim Report of the Mhong Language Council Conference August 12-14, 1982*. Washington, D.C.: Center for Applied Linguistics, 1982.

Thao, Paoze. "Teaching Modals in Mong ESL Classes," MA Departmental Paper,   Northeastern Illinois University, 1985. Unpublished Paper.

Thao, Paoze. "Mong Resettlement in the Chicago Area (1978-1987): Educational Implications, Ph.D. Dissertation, Loyola University of Chicago, 1994.

Thao, Paoze. *Kevcai Siv Lug Moob* [Foundations of Mong Language]. Marina, CA: PT Publishing, 1997.

Thao, Su. *Ncu Txug Tsaj Ntsig Moob I & II* [Commemoration of Mong Veterans], Video-recording, Denver, Colorado, 22 July 1995.   Fresno, California: S.T. Universal Video, 1995 & 1996.

Tsaj, C. *Hmoob Nyob Pa Tawg Teb* [The Hmong in Wenshan]. Guyane France: Association Communaute Hmong, n.d.

Thao, Xeng Pao. "History of the Development of Mong Literacy." Madison Heights, Michigan. Interview. 18 February 1984.

Thao, Xuxu. "The History of Lao Evangelical Church." Ottawa, Illinois. Interview. 1 January 1987.

Thee, Marek. *Notes of a Witness: Laos and the Second Indochinese War.* New York: Vintage Books Edition, 1973.

Thoj, Phaj. *Paaj Lug Moob* [Mong Parables]. Iowa City: Published by the Author, 1982.

Toye, Hugh. *Laos: Buffer State or Battleground.* London: Oxford University Press, 1968.

Trinity-Arlington Teacher and Parent Training for School Success project, Model for Use with limited English proficient High School Students (Arlington Public Schools, 1986), Home Lesson 2 and 6.

Tsaj, Chij. *Hmoob Nyob Pa Tawg Teb* [The Mong in Wenshan]. Guyane France: Association Communaute Hmong, n.d.

U.S. Committee for Refugees. *1981 World Refugee Survey.* Washington, D.C.: U.S. Committee for Refugees, 1981.

U.S. Committee for Refugees. *Refugee Reports.* Vol. X., No. 12. Washington, D.C.: U.S. Committee for Refugees. (December 1991), 10.

U.S. Congress, House, Committee on the Judiciary, *Immigration and Nationality Acts.* H.R. 101st Congress, 1st session. Washington, D.C.: U.S. Government Printing Office, 1989, pp. 313-316.

U.S. Department of Health and Human Services. *Profiles of the Highland Lao Communities in the United States.* Washington, D.C.: Government Printing Office, 1988.

U.S. Department of Justice, Immigration and Naturalization Service. *United States History: 1600-1987.* Washington, D.C.: U.S. Government Printing Office, 1988.

Vang, (General) Pao. Speech at the Hmong's New Year's Day. Des Moines, Iowa. 29 November 1980; and Personal conversation with author, 5-6 January 1981.

Viravong, Maha Sila. *History of Laos.* New York: Paragon Book Reprint Corp., 1964.

Webster, Leila. "Journeys of the Miao." Unpublished Paper, 3 December 1978.

Westermeyer, Joseph. "Hmong Deaths," *Science.* Vol. 213, 1982, p. 952.

White, Peter T. "The Poppy," *National Geographic.* Vol. 16, No. 2. Washington, D.C.: National Geographic Society, February 1985, pp. 143-188.

Wolfkill, Carl. *Reported to Be Alive.* New York: Simon & Schuster, 1965.

Xiong, Lang; Xiong, Joua; and Xiong, Nao Leng. *English-Mong-English Dictionary.* Milwaukee, WI: Hetrick Printing, Inc., 1983.

Xyooj, Xeev Nruag. "Txooj Moob Huv Nplaj Teb," [The Mong in the World], *Txooj Moob.* Vol. 4. Winfield, Illinois: Mong Volunteer Literacy, Inc., May 1989, 8-12.

Yang, Dao. *Les Hmong du Laos au Developpement.* Vientiane: Edition Siaosavath, 1975.

Resources for Mong Language Materials

The following annotated resources have been selected to support mainstream teachers in their continued professional growth in their teaching. It is quite helpful in furthering their knowledge of language learning, literacy, and teaching. However, during the course of this investigation of resources, the finding reveals that there is a great need for the development of bilingual materials in Mong and in English.

After a careful examination of the printed materials for K-12, almost all the resources were written in the White Hmong dialect (Hmong Dawb) ; whereas materials written in Blue Mong (Mong Leng) dialect, for the most part, untouched or neglected by publishers. Therefore, equity is an issue in terms of materials, resources for both Mong dialects. On the other hand, religious materials are available in both Blue Mong and White Hmong. The author found that Christian literacy has been equitably and equally published across the board, such as Sunday School materials and Christian literacy. This initiative was taken by Mong/Hmong Christian leaders to assure that Christian literacy is promoted on a non-discriminatory basis. The Bible Society adopted a bilateral policy on publishing the Bible, hymnal books, and other handbooks in both Blue Mong and White Hmong versions. However, there is a wide gap between printed materials for Blue Mong students in the public schools across the nation. In other words, there are more materials available in White Hmong than Blue Mong. As a result, students who speak Blue Mong dialect have been forced to learn White Hmong dialect. This may potentially create some internal conflict within the Mong society between the Blue Mong and the White Hmong if equity is not promoted by officials of the School Districts across the nation.

In terms of teaching and learning in the classrooms, teachers should be aware that Mong students either speak Blue Mong or White Hmong dialect. The two Mong dialects are spoken by equal numbers of Mong speakers throughout the United States. Though the two Mong dialects seem to be mutually intelligible, this linguistic and ethno-cultural difference is about thirty (30%) percent between the two dialects. Teachers should be sensitive to the fact that there are currently more printed materials in the White Hmong dialect than the Blue Mong's and that students who speak Blue Mong dialect should not be forced to give up their dialect. In the meantime, there should be a balance in the amount of Mong bilingual materials in the classrooms so that teachers could validate their students' linguistic and ethno-cultural groups instead of imposing students coming from one linguistic and ethno-cultural group to learn the materials in one dialect over another.

Please be advised that the list of resources below do not follow the conventional style of the Chicago Manual due to insufficient information. However, the author divides these resources into categories (such as fiction and non-fiction) and by grade level (such as K-3, 3-6 etc.).

Fiction

K-3

Cha, D. *Dia's Story Cloth: The Hmong People's Journey of Freedom*. (K and up). English, 1996.
Mathews, P.B. and Chau, K. *Farmer Boy*. 32 pp. (K-2) English. 1995.
Pfister, M. *The Rainbow Fish*. 32 pp. Hmong English. (K-3), n.d.
Yang, M. *Yer and the Tiger*. 32 pp. English Hmong (K-3). 1981.

2nd to 6th Grades

Coburn, J. R. and O'Brien, A. *Jouanah: A Hmong Cinderella*. 32 pp., English. (All ages). 1996.
Giacchino-Baker, R. *Story of Mah: a Hmong "Romeo and Juliet" Story*. 32 pp. (6-12). 1997.
_____. *Teacher's Resource Book for The Story of Mah*. n.d.
_____. *Teacher's Resource Book for Hmong Culture*. n.d.
_____. *Making connections with Hmong Culture: A Teacher's Resource Book of Thematic Classroom Activities that Promote Intercultural Understanding*. English. 1997.
_____. *Stories from Laos: Folktales and Cultures of the Lao, Hmong, Khammu, and Iu Mien*. 104 pp. (7 & up). English, 1995.
Johnson, C. *Hmong Folk Tales 1 and Hmong Folk Tales 2*. 28 pp. (all ages), 1980.

_____. *Six Hmong Folk Tales*. (6-10), 32 pp., English, 1981.
_____. *Myths, Legends & Folk Tales from the Hmong of Laos*. 520 pp. (6-10), English/Hmong., 1992.

Lee, P. *Vim Leejtwg--* Australia. 196 pp. (all ages). Hmong, 1994.

___. *Neej Kuamuag* -- Australia. 219 pp. (all ages). Hmong, 1994.

___. *Txoj Sawhlub.* -- Australia. 196 pp. (all ages). Hmong, 1987.

___. *Neej Daitaw.* -- Australia. 195pp. (all ages). Hmong, 1986.

Livo, N. and Cha, D. *Folk Stories of the Hmong: Peoples of Laos, Thailand, and Vietnam.* 135 pp. (3 and up), 1991.

Lucas, A. and Kong, K. *How the Farmer Tricked the Evil Demon.* 32 pp. (3-6), 1995.

Pfister, M. *Rainbow Fish to the Rescue.* 32 pp. (K-3). Hmong/English. n.d.

Shea, P. D. *The Whispering Cloth: A Refugee Story.* 32 pp. (3 and up). English, 1995.

Spagnoli, C. and Hom, N. *Nine-in-One Grr! Grr!* 32 pp. (6-12), English, 1989.

Thoj, P. and Thoj, X. P. *Kwv Huam Kaabtshoob Kevkug Moob* [Stories about Courtship and Bride Price]. Winfield, IL: Mong Volunteer Literacy, Inc., 1981.

Thoj, P. et al. *Lug Nruag Dlaab* [Ghost Folktales]. Mong, n.d..

Thoj, P. and Xyooj, X.D. *Lug Nruag Txa* [Transformation Folktales]. Mong, Winfield, IL: Mong Volunteer Literacy, Inc. n.d.

___. *Lug Nruag Tsuv* [Tiger Folktales]. Mong. Winfield, IL: Mong Volunteer Literacy, Inc., (n.d.).

Xiong, I. *The Gift: The Hmong New Year.* 32 pp. (3-6). English/Hmong. 1996.

Yang, M. and Rodriguez, D. *Yer & the Tiger.* 32 pp. (all ages). English/Hmong, 1981.

Non-Fiction

Second to 6th Grades

Caraway, C. *Southeast Asian Textile Designs.* 47 pp. (all ages). English, 1983.

Chan, A. *Hmong Textile Designs.* 42 pp. (All ages). English, 1990.

Pfaff, T. *Hmong in America: Journey From a Secret War.* 100 pp. 13 and up). English, 1995.

Roling, M.A. & Staton, D. *Beginning Word Book.* 154 pp. (all ages). English/Hmong, 1989.

Livo, N.J. and Cha, D. *Folk Stories of the Hmong: Peoples of Laos, Thailand, and Vietnam.* Englewood, CO: Libraries Unlimited. 135 pp. (8 & up), English, 1991.
Shea, P. D. & Riggio, A. *Whispering Cloth: A Refugee's Story.* Honesdale, PA: Boyds Mills. 32 pp. (6-10). English, 1995.
Xyooj, X. D. and Thoj, T.K. (1981). *Kawm Ntawv Moob Phoo 1* [Learning Mong Book 1]. Mong. Winfield, IL: Mong Volunteer Literacy, Inc., 1981.
Xyooj, X.D. *Lub Neej Ib Vuag Dlua* [Past Experience]. Mong. Winfield, IL: Mong Volunteer Literacy, Inc., n.d.

Fiction

7th Grades and Up

Giacchino-Baker, R. *Stories from Laos: Folktales and Cultures of the Lao, Hmong, Khammu, and Iu Mien.* 104 pp. (7 and up), 1995.
Willcox, D. *Hmong Folklife.* 116 pp. (15 & up). English, 1986.

Non-Fiction

7th Grades and up

Chang, K. and Pinkel, S. *Kou Chang's Story.* 127 pp. (10 & up), 1993.
Chang, S. *Hmong Means Free: Life in Laos and America,* n.d.
Donnelly, N. D. *Changing Lives of Refugee Hmong Women.* 224 pp. (7 & up). English, 1994.
Goldfarb, M. *Fighters, Refugees, Immigrants.* 40 pp. (12-16). English, 1982.
Hmong Youth Cultural Awareness Project. *A Free People: Our Stories, Our Voices, Our Dreams.* , 144 pp. (9 and up). English, 1994.

Hamilton-Merritt, J. *Tragic Mountain: the Hmong, the Americans, and the Wars for Laos, 1942-1992.* 448 pp. (6 & up). English, 1993.
Heimbach, E.*White Hmong-English Dictionary.* 497 pp. (all ages). English/Hmong, 1979.
Hoyt, L. and Goudvis, A. *Young Hmong Voices.* 53 pp. (12 & up). English/Hmong, 1997.
Lewis, P. and Lewis, E. *Peoples of the Golden Triangle.* 200 pp. (15 & up). English, 1980.
Lewis, J. *Minority Cultures of Laos: Kamu, Lua', Lahu, Hmong*

and Iu Mien. 401 pp. (9 & up). English, 1992.
Mattison, W.; Lo, L. and Scarseth, T. *Hmong Lives, From Laos to La Crosse.* 205 pp., 1994.
Miller, S. L. *Hmong Voices in Montana.* 144 pp. (11 and up). English, 1992.
Moore, P. H. *The Hmong: Yesterday & Today.* 72 pp. (15 & up). English, 1987.
Pfaff, T. *Hmong in America: Journey from a Secret War.* 100 pp. English, 1995.
Thoj, X.P. and Xyooj, X. D. *Kawm Ntawv Moob Phoo 2* [Learning Mong, Book 2]. Mong. Winfield, IL: Mong Volunteer Literacy, Inc., 1984.
_____. *Phoo/Phau Kawm Koom, Moob Leeg/Hmoob Dawb* [Learning Mong Leng/Hmong Dawb]. Mong Leng/Hmong Dawb. Winfield, IL: Mong Volunteer Literacy, Inc., 1984. n.d.
Thoj, X. P. *Paajlug Moob* [Mong Proverbs]. Mong. Winfield, IL: Mong Volunteer Literacy, Inc., 1983.
_____. *Phoo Qha Siv Lu Lug Meej hab Tsi Meej* [How to Use Mong Minimal Pairs]. Mong. Winfield, IL: Mong Volunteer Literacy, Inc., 1982.
Vang, L. & Lewis, J. *Grandmother's Path, Grandfather's Way.* 190 pp. (12 & up). English/Hmong. Rancho Cordova, CA: Southeast Asian Community Resource Center, 1990.
Warner, R.. *Tawm Lostsus Mus* [Out of Laos: A Story of War and Exodus, Told in Photographs]. English/Hmong. Rancho Cordova, CA: Southeast Asian Community Resource Center, n.d.
Xyooj, X. D. and Thoj, T.K. *Kawm Ntawv Moob Phoo 1* [Learning Mong Book 1]. Mong. Winfield, IL: Mong Literacy Volunteer, Inc., 1981.

Higher Education - Non-Fiction

Bliatout, B. T. et al. *Handbook for Teaching Hmong-Speaking Students.* 129 pp. English. Rancho Cordova, CA: Southeast Asia Community Resource Center, 1988.
Lewis, P. and Lewis, E. *Peoples of the Golden Triangle.* 200 pp. (15 & up). English. Great Britain: Thames and Hudson, Ltd., 1984.
Lewis, J. *Minority Cultures of Laos: Kammu, Lua', Lahu, Hmong, and Iu Mien.* ed. 402 pp. English. Rancho Cordova, CA: Southeast Asia Community Resource Center, 1992.
Moore, P. H. *The Hmong: Yesterday & Today.* 72 pp. (15 & up). English. 1987.

Pfaff, T. *Hmong in America: Journey from a Secret War.* 100 pp.
    English. Eau Claire, WI: Chippewa Valley Museum Press,
    1995.
Smalley, W. A. *Linguistic Diversity and National Unity:
    Language Ecology in Thailand.* Chicago, IL: The University
    of Chicago Press. 436 pp. English, 1994.
Smalley, W.A. et al. *Mother of Writing: The Origin and
    Development of a Hmong Messianic Script.* Chicago, IL:
    The University of Chicago Press. 221 pp. English, 1990.
Te, H. D. and Vang, L. *English-Hmong Bilingual Dictionary of
    School Terminology.* [Cov Lus Mis Kuj Txhais ua Lus
    Hmoob]. Hmong. Rancho Cordova, CA: Southeast Asia
    Community Resource Center, 1988.
Te, H.D. *Helping Your Child Achieve in School: A Handbook
    for Southeast Asian Parents.* 64pp. English. Rancho
    Cordova, CA: Southeast Asian Culture and Education
    Foundation, 1996.
Thao, Paoze *Kevcai Siv Lug Moob* [Foundations of Mong
    Language]. 124 pp. (15 & up). Marina, CA:PT Publishing,
    1997. Mong.
Trueba, H. T. *Cultural Conflict and Adaptatioin: The Case of
    Hmong Children in American Society.* 157 pp. (15 & up)
    United Kingdom: The Falmer Press, 1990.
Walker, W. *An Introduction to the Hmong.* 20 pp. English,
    1989.
Warner, R. *Tawm Lostsus Mus* [Out of Laos: A Story of War and
    Exodus, Told in Photographs]. English/Hmong. Rancho
    Cordova, CA: Southeast Asia Community Resource Center,
    n.d.

Index

ABOUT THE AUTHOR

Paoze Thao, one of the pioneer faculty for the Center for Collaborative Education and Professional Studies, California State University, Monterey Bay, received his B.Ed. from Chulalongkorn University (Bangkok, Thailand) in 1976, M.A. in Applied Linguistics from Northeastern Illinois University in 1986, and Ph.D. from Loyola University of Chicago in Historical Foundations of Education in 1994. He served as a Training and Research Specialist for the Multifunctional Resource Center for Bilingual Education, College of Education, University of Wisconsin – Madison from 1993-1995; Director of Outreach for the U.S. Department of Justice, Immigration and Naturalization Service, Chicago District from 1987-1992, and as Supervisor of the Multi-Ethnic units of Travelers and Immigrants Aid in Chicago from 1978-1987. Dr. Thao, the first Mong-American who was awarded Ph.D. degree in Education in the United States, writes in the areas of applied linguistics and historical and comparative education. Dr. Thao was among the very few Mong-American scholars in the field of education.